VIRGINIA
1584-1607

3

TO THE RIGHT
WORTHIE AND HONOV-
RABLE, SIR VVALTER RALEGH,
KNIGHT, SENESCHAL OF THE DVCHIES OF
Cornewall and Exeter, and L. Warden of the ſtannaries in Deuon
and Cornewall. T.B. wiſheth true felicie.

AMORE ET VIRTVTE.

I R, ſeeing that the parte of the Worlde, which is betwene the
FLORIDA and the Cap BRETON nowe nammed VIRGI-
NIA, to the honneur of yours moſt ſouueraine Layde and Queene ELIZABETZ, hath ben deſcouuerd by yours meanes. And
great chardges. And that your Collonye hath been theer eſtab-
liſhed to your great honnor and prayſe, and noe leſſer proffit vnto the common

A 2

DEDICATION FROM HARIOT'S BRIEFE AND TRUE REPORT

VIRGINIA
1584-1607

THE FIRST ENGLISH SETTLEMENT
IN NORTH AMERICA

A BRIEF HISTORY WITH A SELECTION
OF CONTEMPORARY NARRATIVES

EDITED BY ALAN SMITH, B.A.

THEODORE BRUN
FINE EDITIONS LIMITED
LONDON

VIRGINIA PUBLICATIONS

FIRST PUBLISHED 1957
BY
THEODORE BRUN
FINE EDITIONS LIMITED
31 EYRE STREET HILL,
LONDON, E.C.1.

Made and printed in Great Britain

Photo-litho Plates and print
by Edwards & Brune Ltd.
31 Eyre Street Hill,
London, E.C.1

To the memory of
Sir Walter Raleigh, Captain John Smith
and the other brave adventurers
who planted the first British Colonies
in North America

PREFACE AND ACKNOWLEDGMENTS

The Contemporary Narratives and a number of illustrations in this book have been reproduced from Richard Hakluyt's *The Principal Navigations*, (Vol. VIII), *Voyages, Traffiques & Discoveries of the English Nation*, and Captain John Smith's *The Generall Historie of Virginia, New England & The Summer Isles*. We wish to thank here the publishers, Messrs. Jackson, Son & Co Ltd, Glasgow, for their generous permission to make extracts from the two volumes and to reproduce them by photo-litho process.

Richard Hakluyt's "Principal Navigations" were first published in London in 1589; John Smith's "Generall Historie" in 1624. Messrs. Jackson's editions—published under the imprint of their predecessors James MacLehose and Sons for the University of Glasgow—appeared in 1904 and 1907 respectively. They are an exact reprint of the Original Editions except that the letters i, j, u and v have been altered to conform to modern usage, and obvious printers' errors, both of spelling and punctuation, have been corrected. We have been very happy to use these texts which are faithful to the originals without being cumbersome to modern eyes.

Variations in spelling, especially of names, occur frequently in both books; there are sometimes slight discrepancies in the narratives; these observations are mentioned just in passing: we felt no need to burden the book with heavy foot notes. No alterations have been made in the original text. Omissions are indicated by a series of dots . . .

From Richard Hakluyt's "Principal Navigations" we have taken the following Narratives: The First Voyage to Virginia; The Second Voyage to Virginia; Ralph Lane's Letter to Richard Hakluyt; Ralph Lane's Report from Virginia; The Third Voyage to Virginia; Thomas Harriot's Report from Virginia; John White's Letter to Richard Hakluyt.

From John Smith's "Generall Historie": The Fourth Voyage to Virginia; The Fifth Voyage to Virginia; Captain Gosnoll's Report; The Landing in Virginia; The Pocahontas Story; Letter to the Council of Virginia; Lord de la Ware's Arrival.

We are indebted to the British Museum for the permission to reproduce a number of De Bry's engravings; to the Public Record Office for the permission to reproduce the Round Robin.

Last but not least we wish to express our particular thanks to friends of the English Speaking Union who gave us the most generous help in the production of the book.

Contents

LIST OF ILLUSTRATIONS

INTRODUCTION

HIS year the English-speaking peoples celebrate the three hundred and fiftieth anniversary of the founding of Jamestown, the first permanent English colony on the North American continent, and this book tells the Jamestown story. It is an adventure story and is frankly presented as such, but although the story we tell here ends in 1610 with Lord Delaware's final, fantastic, last minute salvation of the Jamestown venture, the story of Jamestown does not end there. Jamestown was a seed planted in the virgin soil of a new enticing continent.

The Virginia colony was a lure that drew many men and ships across the wide Atlantic. The ten week passage into the unknown, (ten weeks that is, if the weather was good) seemed to the men of those times almost as a flight to the moon would seem to us. And, as will doubtless be the case with the first interplanetary voyagers, many of the early shots went wide.

The Bermudas were first discovered in 1609 when a ship seeking Virginia was driven miles off her course, and in 1620 the Pilgrim Fathers founded their settlement at Plymouth only because the captain of the Mayflower, having made his landfall hundreds of miles too far north, was unwilling to risk his chances against the shoals and breakers of the coast in attempting to work down to Chesapeake Bay, their intended destination. And so, by time and chance, these men were brought to that place, and the whole future of North America and her new inhabitants was cast in a mould that could not be broken.

1619 too was a fateful year for Virginia and for America, for in that year the first American representative assembly met in Jamestown Church, twenty-two burgesses chosen from the plantations to assist the Governor in the administration of the colony, and, more fateful still, twenty African slaves were sold in Jamestown for plantation labour.

By 1620 40,000 tons of tobacco had already been shipped to England. A new industry had been born. Any large scale efforts at mixed farming for subsistence crops soon went by the board, as did the fond hopes of the Virginia Company that the colony would supply "all the commodities of Europe, Africa and Asia" as well as remedying the wants of "all our decayed trades." (In a similarly optimistic vein, Oglethorpe, when he established Georgia in 1733, thought that the principal products of the settlement there ought to be wine and silk. Georgia, like Virginia, did not oblige.) Plantations, growing one staple crop—tobacco, indigo, sugar and later cotton—all alike in that they were easily tended by unskilled labour, became the dominant unit of production.

Tobacco had been known in England long before, having been imported from the Spanish colonies, but until John Rolfe, of whom we shall hear much more in this story, devised a method of curing tobacco that pleased the English palate, Virginian tobacco could find no ready sale in the Mother Country. Rolfe found such a method and the tobacco industry throve. By 1620 the industry was becoming important, the cured leaf fetching five shillings a pound in London. The soil was fertile (in this at least the Virginia Company's prospectus had spoken no more than the sober truth), black labour readily available and the economic incentives great. Eventually over-production resulted and the Virginia planters, as years went by, fell deeper and deeper into debt with the merchants of London. These debts they often bequeathed to their sons and thus was sown one of the seeds of trans-Atlantic discontent that was eventually to grow into a war for independence. The roots of American history go deep and nowhere deeper than in Virginia.

Jamestown, like Plymouth, had been planted by a commercial concern, a Chartered Company organised for profit, and between 1606 and 1621 the Virginia Company poured £100,000 into the colony and though the shareholders held doggedly on until 1632, long after the colony itself had reverted to the Crown, no dividend was ever paid. The sealed orders given to the first settlers had recommended that while two-thirds of them should be employed in establishing the actual settlement, the rest should press on to the major objectives—gold and a passage to the South Sea. Virginia's tobacco wealth was neither sought for nor expected, the mass influx of slaves was never contemplated in the beginning, but these factors, combined with others that were the product of intention, all became ingredients in the making of the old South that went down in the War between the States. As the oak is in the acorn, awaiting only fertilisation and time to draw it forth, so the South was all in Jamestown, ready to emerge by natural stages of growth.

The Virginian colony rapidly became a land of great estates. Before dissolving itself and surrendering its lands to the Crown the Virginia Company voted big tracts of land to its officials and certain of its shareholders and by accepting the institution of "head-rights" the royal government confirmed this trend to big holdings. From 1618 onwards, anyone who emigrated to Virginia at his own expense could claim fifty acres of land not only for himself but for any members of his party and for any subsequent immigrant whose passage money he paid, provided only that in a reasonable time the land was cleared and at least nominally occupied. The system lent itself to the building of huge estates by vigorous and enterprising characters and by the middle of the next century estates of ten thousand acres and upward had become common.

When King James granted their foundation charter to the London Company (for that was the first name of the Virginia Company) giving permission for them to attempt their settlement in the New World, he insisted that the colonists should be Englishmen and that the Established Church of England should be the religion of the colony; so it was only with some misgivings that he a few years later gave permission for a party of English "Separatists" (a small ultra-Puritan denomination) at that time voluntarily exiled in the Netherlands city of Leyden to go over and establish another colony in English America. He was however prevailed upon to do so. A syndicate of London merchants put up seven thousand pounds. The Virginia Company indicated Chesapeake Bay as a suitable place for the new landing and the Separatists, numbering one hundred-and-two put to sea in the Mayflower in September 1620.

As we have seen, the Mayflower never made Chesapeake Bay coming to anchor instead in what the maps now show as Provincetown harbour. So, by sheer chance, what should have been an addition of strength to the first colony became in fact an alternative bridgehead for immigrants, and one very different in character from Jamestown. The financing syndicate became the Plymouth Company. The Plymouth colony was born: the "Pilgrim Fathers" were established in America: a new seed was set in America's soil. A single friendly Indian, Samasett, appeared and told the settlers of another Indian, Squanto, who could speak good English and had, indeed, been to England. Squanto was the sole survivor of the local Indians who had, it seemed, been wiped out by a plague. Squanto stayed with the settlers and instructed them in the local farming lore. They planted corn and vegetables. Their first winter was a hard one. Their corn and beans saved them, for their skill in hunting and fishing was pitifully inadequate, yet not all could be saved, for by the spring, when the Mayflower sailed home, only fifty were left alive of the hundred and two who had landed in December.

As winter approached again, the arrival of thirty new settlers, without any food supplies, proved a nearly insupportable burden but somehow they got through the bad weather. In the spring (1622) more than sixty new settlers, again without food, arrived and the summer, long awaited as a time of relative abundance, was a season of famine. The Plymouth colony was never either big or important. Its life as a separate entity was only a short one for in 1691 it was absorbed by the larger colony of Massachusetts Bay. Its significance was that it provided a focus for a new immigration and grew into a society quite different from that evolving in the South. New England, for that is what the northern settlements became, was a land of hard winters and difficult farming. The farming was mixed in character, demanding skilled labour and having no use for slaves. There was no single crop around which a whole economy was built as in the South. The coast lands, to which the colonists were confined, were narrow, timber however was abundant and great fishing grounds lay not far from the shore: the New Englanders took to the sea. They became fishermen, then shipbuilders, then the commerce carriers of the whole of British North America. Shipbuilding demanded skilled craftsmen and so, when in later years, the water power flowing down the hillsides was harnessed to industry, all the elements of a factory economy were ready to hand.

Jamestown and Plymouth were the twin roots of the U.S.A. and every factor, whether of chance or of intention, served to emphasise the gulf between them. During the early reign of Charles 1st, when the pressure of orthodoxy was again heavy upon the Puritans, some twenty thousand of them, from Eastern and South-Eastern England, moved into the Massachusetts region. When the Puritans gained control in England, their outflow ceased and Virginia was given a great increase in strength by an influx of English Royalist sympathisers.

Jamestown and Plymouth, the twin nuclei of English settlement in North America, each developed a characteristic and contrasting society New England was a land of small farms and working farmers, the South of large slave-run plantations. In the North, once the settlers had broken out from the coast-lands, the trend was for property to be divided between children. In the South, the large land unit, not to be broken up without serious economic inconvenience, led to inheritance by the eldest son and the establishment of entails becoming the prevailing custom. In the North, the compact villages witnessed to the corporate spirit of the congregations of the 'pilgrims' and soon grew into flourishing townships. The South remained predominantly rural—and aristocratic—to the very last. There the county was the unit of administration.

Slavery was the outstanding feature of Southern civilisation. It produced a leisured class of proprietors who inevitably grew to despise manual labour and who therefore were hardly likely to display any technical inventiveness Slavery was, in hard fact, uneconomic and a burden on the society that upheld it The lines of fatality run through the whole story. Sir Walter Ralegh dreamed of an English nation in far away Virginia; John Rolfe learned how to cure tobacco; twenty negroes, offered for sale in little Jamestown, found ready purchasers; the Mayflower sails to Cape Cod instead of to Chesapeake. When the first colonies were established, the inevitable future separation was perhaps to be discerned. When the year 1620 saw two colonies on the mainland instead of one, the crushing of 'the gallant South' in the War between the States was quite as inevitably programmed by History. But how did it all begin? Why did Ralegh dream of a new English nation beyond the seas? And why was Virginia the chosen ground for this inspired doom-burdened experiment.

Probably the first English ships to sail along the coasts of Ralegh's Virginia were those of John Cabot in 1498, and although it has been rightly said by a learned commentator that on this voyage Cabot sailed 'out of precisely recorded history', some general idea of his attainment is not beyond conjecture. Cabot (and he was not, of course, alone in this) did not yet realise the true nature of America. He took it to be an outlying part of the continent of Asia and, it would seem, planned to coast down it to the tropics where he would find both the island of Cipangu (Japan) and the mainland territories of Cathay. On his first (1497) voyage Cabot had touched America at a northerly point, either in Newfoundland or perhaps Nova Scotia, had coasted far enough to establish that his discovery was no mere island and had then returned. This contact had opened up the Newfoundland fishing grounds for England but Cabot had more ambitious plans in contemplation. On his second voyage therefore, he went back to his first landfall and proceeded southwards even further than before. How far south he actually got we cannot say for certain, but two tantalisingly obscure pieces of evidence give us reason to believe that he came down to the tropics he sought for. In 1499 a Spanish sailor named Alonso de Hojeda had been voyaging off the coast of Venezuela. In June 1501 the King and Queen of Spain commissioned him to return to those coasts, to follow them "setting up marks with the arms of their Majesties" in order to forestall the English who were known to be making discoveries in some not too distant region. Further, the map of America compiled by the Spaniard de la Cosa in 1500 (some would prefer the date 1509) undoubtedly shows a long western coastline dotted with English flags.

However, whatever Cabot actually did discover, it was neither Cathay nor Cipangu. A barrier, formidable in size, lay sprawled between the Atlantic and the wealth of the Indies. The next English endeavours in the New World were for the most part directed to finding a way round it. In the South the Spaniards had gold and silver to sweeten their disappointment. To the Northerners America was a frustration and a mockery.

Besides being the first English expedition to explore in North America Cabot's venture touches the Jamestown story at yet another point. The fact is recorded that, in connection with Cabot's 1498 voyage, the King, Henry VII, had promised a contingent of convicts for use as heavy labour in the foundation of a colony. There is no evidence that these men were ever embarked, or that any attempt was ever actually made to establish a colony, but it is plain that the plan was under consideration. Presumably the colony would have been in what Cabot thought were the barren lands of Northern Asia, to be used in connection with the fisheries or perhaps as a halfway house for the hoped for trade with tropical Asia. We need not suppose that either Cabot or King Henry were contemplating the penetration of Cathay itself.

In December 1502 Henry issued another patent, this time to a syndicate of Bristol merchants, authorising further explorations, and again it is plain that permanent colonies were envisaged. The syndicate made voyages until at least 1505 but we do not know where to nor whether they ever took up their colonial aims in earnest.

The next phase of important European penetration was centred on more southerly territories, for on Easter Sunday 1513, Ponce de Leon touched land on the northern margin of the Caribbean Sea. In Spanish Easter Sunday is 'Pascua Florida' so the name of Florida was given to the new territory. For the Spaniards, their new claims extended from New Mexico and the Gulf in the south right up to the very Pole and many vain attempts were made to secure their title of discovery by taking actual possession. So disastrous were these efforts that in September 1561, Phillip II forbade any further attempts to occupy the East coast. He was quite unaware that almost at that very moment a French expedition to Florida was being prepared.

It was the eve of the French Wars of Religion; the power of the French Huguenots was as yet unbroken and their leader, the Admiral Coligny, was desirous of strengthening their position still further by the establishment of overseas settlements. There had been an abortive attempt to do this in 1555, the chosen ground being Brazil. Florida, however, offered a much more enticing prospect, for whoever dominated the Florida Strait would have the Spanish treasure fleets at their mercy. In 1562 then, two Huguenot ships set sail from Havre de Grace for Florida. They arrived off what is now St. Augustine on April 30th, sailed up the coast annexing land in the name of France and establishing 'Charlesfort' near the present Beaufort, South Carolina. Thirty men were left to hold this new outpost of France while Ribaut, the commander of the expedition, set sail again for France promising to return with supplies in six months time. Meanwhile the Frenchmen completed their little fortifications, made contacts with the Indians, hunted and went fishing, but made no attempt to start any cultivation of their own; they had their supplies and Ribaut would soon return. But Ribaud never came. On reaching France he had become involved in the Civil War then raging between Catholics and Protestants and was unable to organise the relieving expedition he had promised. In Florida meanwhile the little band was growing desperate. Food was getting scarce, the fort was destroyed by fire and the little company was torn by mutiny. The captain Ribaud had set in charge was murdered and a new one, Barré,

XVIII

chosen in his place. Still no relief came and their plight grew even worse. Deciding to venture all on one last gamble they built a crazy boat and took to the sea, but they fared there even worse than on the land, being reduced to cannibalism before they were finally rescued by an English ship.

Now the news of France's challenge to Spain was revealed to the world and Spain's reaction was sudden and furious. A small, but adequate force was sent to Florida, the surviving physical remains of the French settlement were obliterated and the Spaniards returned to Havana. Ribaut however had not forgotten Florida. He was now in England, a refugee after the fall to the Catholics of Huguenot-held Dieppe, had had an audience with Queen Elizabeth, and published in May 1563 a book about his voyage to Florida. An English adventurer, Thomas Stukeley, was discussing a joint expedition with Ribaut when the latter suddenly changed his attitude, perhaps fearing that he was merely used by the English, and attempted to flee the country. But in those days no one under the jurisdiction of England's Queen was permitted to come and go as he pleased, and Ribaut was too highly valued. He was imprisoned in the Tower of London and was there when the survivors of his 'Charlesfort' settlement were brought to England. All these events served to excite English interest in Florida and to draw English eyes away from the North of the continent, the traditional field of English enterprise in America.

The war in France having come to a temporary standstill, Admiral Coligny resolved to challenge Spain for a second time. Accordingly, on April 22nd 1564, three ships sailed again from Havre de Grace. Eight weeks later they sighted the shores of Florida and dropped anchor just to the north of the St. Johns River. Contacts with the Indians were renewed, a fort, Fort Caroline, was erected. The fate of this settlement, though different, was no happier than that of the first. The settlers became embroiled in Indian wars and rumours of gold in the mountains broke down discipline. The colony was weakened by desertions and the Spaniards came to know of its existence. Eventually Ribaut himself, eventually released by the English, came again from France to take over command and his arrival kindled fresh hope in the settlers.

The end of the French colony was however in sight; a Spanish fleet arrived, drove off Ribaut's waiting ships and then turned south to establish the fort that grew into the city of St. Augustine. From then onwards it was open war. The French ships came back and joined in the fighting, but to no avail. Fort Caroline was destroyed with heavy loss of life. One of the French ships was wrecked and a party of survivors massacred. Eventually the rest of the French forces—with their commander—were forced to surrender and they, too, were massacred. In

1567 a French Catholic, De Gourgues, led a punitive raid on Fort Mateo, as the Spanish had renamed Fort Caroline, massacring all its defenders, but this was the last effort of the French in Florida. They had no more heart for the struggle. England, however, was beginning to stir again.

Obsessed with the desire to follow in the track of Cabot, and burning with zeal to find new wealth for Britain beyond the seas, Sir Humphrey Gilbert had in 1566 asked the Queen for permission to organise a voyage in search of the North West Passage. Leave had not been granted and Gilbert found himself sent on royal business to Ireland instead. Eight years passed and Gilbert persisted in his dreaming, presenting to the Queen in 1574 his "Discourse to prove a Passage by the North West to Cathaia". Once again his efforts availed him nought and it was to Martin Frobisher that the Royal Licence to seek the North West Passage was eventually given. It is, however, the "Discourse" that brings onto the stage "that rare and renowned knight" Sir Walter Ralegh. Ralegh was Gilbert's half-brother and he is conjectured by some to have had a hand in the writing of the "Discourse". Certainly Gilbert was one of the earliest to see, and publicise, the economic value of colonies, the cause with which Ralegh is so intimately associated. Suddenly, on June 11th 1578 the Queen granted Gilbert all he was asking for, issuing him with a Patent which authorised him to "discover, finde, searche out, and view such remote, heathen and barbarous lands . . . as to him . . . shall seem good . . ." He was moreover authorised to establish colonies, and the expedition, at long last realised, set off in the following September. The voyage was an ill-omened one. Beaten back by the weather they set off again only to be attacked by Spaniards off Cape Verde. The scattered fleet crawled into Plymouth demoralised. The first Ralegh-Gilbert venture was defeated.

Gilbert was forced by his financial losses into semi-retirement; Ralegh, on the other hand, was at the beginning of his long and dazzling career. He did not forget Gilbert or the dream of English colonies beyond the seas, and it was he who prevailed upon the Queen to let Gilbert, despite the reputation he had acquired as 'a man of no good hap at sea', sail again to America. Furthermore, he spent two thousand pounds in equipping for the expedition a two hundred ton vessel, the "Ark Ralegh." Gilbert sailed at last and in 1583 annexed Newfoundland, the chosen ground for Britain's first colony.

On the homeward voyage however, Gilbert's ship, the tiny ten ton "Squirrel" was lost with all hands. Gilbert's last moving cry to the men of the "Squirrel's" consort, "We are as near to Heaven by sea as by land", reveals him in his most favourable aspect, 'a soldier, resolute in Christ'.

The cross roads of destiny had now been reached. Had Ralegh decided

INTRODUCTION

to withdraw from colonial projects altogether, his decision would have been an understandable one. Sir Humphrey's brother, Adrian Gilbert, together with John Davis, yet another Devon man, had formed "The Colleagues of the Discovery of the North West Passage" and were pressing for the transfer of Gilbert's Patent to them. Ralegh, however, did not give up. He had dreamed of an English settlement beyond the seas. All through his life he kept the faith that such a colony would be established and that he would "live to see it an English nation".

Because Ralegh dreamed his dream, because he poured out his money and his genius to make it a reality, he blazed the trail for the Jamestown pioneers.

On March 25th 1584 Ralegh received his Letters Patent in terms similar to those given to Gilbert. The whole unoccupied coast of America was his to plant with colonies that he might hold for ever. Like Gilbert he had six years in which to stake his claims. Ralegh took up the challenge. On his initiative and with his financial backing, Englishmen went to the New World, not as hitherto, merely to prospect or to plunder, but to make it their home, a new England beyond the seas. What they found there, what they saw, and what befell them will be told by contemporary narratives on the pages that follow.

Hainault, Essex.   ALAN SMITH
February 1957.

"As in the arts and sciences, the first invention is of more consequence than all the improvements afterward, so, in kingdoms, the first foundation or plantation is of more noble dignity and merit than all that followeth".

Bacon.

1584

THE FIRST VOYAGE TO VIRGINIA

The first voyage made to the coasts of America,
with two barks, where in were Captaines M.
Philip Amadas, and M. Arthur Barlowe, who
discovered part of the Countrey now called
Virginia, Anno 1584. Written by one of the
said Captaines, and sent to sir Walter Ralegh
knight, at whose charge and direction, the
said voyage was set forth.

He 27 day of Aprill, in the yeere of our
redemption, 1584 we departed the West
of England, with two barkes well furnished with men and victuals, having
received our last and perfect directions
by your letters, confirming the former
instructions, and commandements de-
livered by your selfe at our leaving the river of Thames.

The tenth of May we arrived at the Canaries, and the
tenth of June in this present yeere, we were fallen with
the Islands of the West Indies, keeping a more South-
easterly course then was needefull, because wee doubted
that the current of the Bay of Mexico, disbogging betweene the Cape of Florida and Havana, had bene of

greater force then afterwardes we found it to bee. At
which Islands we found the ayre very unwholsome, and
our men grew for the most part ill disposed: so that
having refreshed our selves with sweet water, & fresh
victuall, we departed the twelfth day of our arrivall there.
These Islands, with the rest adjoyning, are so well knowen
to your selfe, and to many others, as I will not trouble
you with the remembrance of them.

The second of July, we found shole water, wher we
smelt so sweet, and so strong a smel, as if we had, bene
in the midst of some delicate garden abounding with all
kinde of odoriferous flowers, by which we were assured,
that the land could not be farre distant: and keeping good
watch, and bearing but slacke saile, the fourth of the same
moneth we arrived upon the coast, which we supposed to
be a continent and firme lande, and we sayled along the
same a hundred and twentie English miles before we
could finde any entrance, or river issuing into the Sea.
The first that appeared unto us, we entred, though not
without some difficultie, & cast anker about three harquebuz-shot within the havens mouth, on the left hand of
the same: and after thankes given to God for our safe
arrivall thither, we manned our boats, and went to view
the land next adjoyning, and " to take possession of the
same, in the right of the Queenes most excellent Majestie,
as rightfull Queene, and Princesse of the same, and after
delivered the same over to your use, according to her
Majesties grant, and letters patents, under her Highnesse
great Seale. Which being performed, according to the
ceremonies used in such enterprises, we viewed the land
about us, being, whereas we first landed, very sandie and
low towards the waters side, but so full of grapes, as the
very beating and surge of the Sea overflowed them, of
which we found such plentie, as well there as in all places
else, both on the sand and on the greene soile on the hils,
as in the plaines, as well on every little shrubbe, as also
climing towards the tops of high Cedars, that I thinke in
all the world the like abundance is not to be found: and

my selfe having seene those parts of Europe that most abound, find such difference as were incredible to be written.

We passed from the Sea side towardes the toppes of those hilles next adjoyning, being but of meane higth, and from thence wee behelde the Sea on both sides to the North, and to the South, finding no ende any of both wayes. This lande lay stretching it selfe to the West, which after wee found to bee but an Island of twentie miles long, and not above sixe miles broade. Under the banke or hill whereon we stoode, we behelde the vallyes replenished with goodly Cedar trees, and having discharged our harquebuz-shot, such a flocke of Cranes (the most part white) arose under us, with such a cry redoubled by many ecchoes, as if an armie of men had showted all together.

This Island had many goodly woodes full of Deere, Conies, Hares, and Fowle, even in the middest of Summer in incredible abundance. The woodes are not such as you finde in Bohemia, Moscovia, or Hercynia, barren and fruitles, but the highest and reddest Cedars of the world, farre bettering the Ceders of the Açores, of the Indies, or Lybanus, Pynes, Cypres, Sassaphras, the Lentisk, or the tree that beareth the Masticke, the tree that beareth the rine of blacke Sinamon, of which Master Winter brought from the streights of Magellan, and many other of excellent smell and qualitie. We remained by the side of this Island two whole dayes before we saw any people of the Countrey: the third day we espied one small boate rowing towardes us having in it three persons: this boat came to the Island side, foure harquebuz-shot from our shippes, and there two of the people remaining, the third came along the shoreside towards us, and wee being then all within boord, he walked up and downe upon the point of the land next unto us: then the Master and the Pilot of the Admirall, Simon Ferdinando, and the Captaine Philip Amadas, my selfe, and others rowed to the land, whose comming this fellow attended, never making any

shewe of feare or doubt. And after he had spoken of
many things not understood by us, we brought him
with his owne good liking, aboord the ships, and gave
him a shirt, a hat & some other things, and made him
taste of our wine, and our meat, which he liked very
wel: and after having viewed both barks, he departed,
and went to his owne boat againe, which hee had left
in a little Cove or Creeke adjoyning: assoone as hee
was two bow shoot into the water, he fell to fishing,
and in lesse then halfe an houre, he had laden his
boate as deepe, as it could swimme, with which hee
came againe to the point of the lande, and there he
devided his fish into two parts, pointing one part to
the ship, and the other to the pinnesse: which, after
he had (as much as he might) requited the former
benefites received, departed out of our sight.

The next day there came unto us divers boates, and
in one of them the Kings brother, accompanied with
fortie or fiftie men, very handsome and goodly people,
and in their behaviour as mannerly and civill as any of
Europe. His name was Granganimeo, and the king is
called Wingina, the countrey Wingandacoa, and now by
her Majestie Virginia. The maner of his comming was
in this sort: hee left his boates altogether as the first
man did a little from the shippes by the shore, and
came along to the place over against the ships,
followed with fortie men. When he came to the place,
his servants spread a long matte upon the ground, on
which he sate downe, and at the other ende of the matte
foure others of his companie did the like, the rest of
his men stood round about him, somewhat a farre off:
when we came to the shore to him with our weapons,
hee never mooved from his place, nor any of the other
foure, nor never mistrusted any harme to be offred
from us, but sitting still he beckoned us to come and
sit by him, which we performed: and being set hee
made all signes of joy and welcome, striking on his head
and his breast and afterwardes on ours, to shewe wee

A VIRGINIAN WARRIOR

5

were all one, smiling and making shewe the best he could of all love, and familiaritie. After hee had made a long speech unto us, wee presented him with divers things, which hee received very joyfully, and thankefully. None of the company durst speake one worde all the time: onely the foure which were at the other ende, spake one in the others eare very softly.

The King is greatly obeyed, and his brothers and children reverenced: the King himselfe in person was at our being there, sore wounded in a fight which hee had with the King of the next countrey, called Wingina, and was shot in two places through the body, and once cleane through the thigh, but yet he recovered: by reason whereof and for that hee lay at the chiefe towne of the countrey, being sixe dayes journey off, we saw him not at all.

After we had presented this his brother with such things as we thought he liked, wee likewise gave somewhat to the other that sat with him on the matte: but presently he arose and tooke all from them and put it into his owne basket, making signes and tokens, that all things ought to bee delivered unto him, and the rest were but his servants, and followers. A day or two after this, we fell to trading with them, exchanging some things that we had, for Chamoys, Buffe, and Deere skinnes: when we shewed him all our packet of merchandize, of all things that he sawe, a bright tinne dish most pleased him, which hee presently tooke up and clapt it before his breast, and after made a hole in the brimme thereof and hung it about his necke, making signes that it would defende him against his enemies arrowes: for those people maintaine a deadly and terrible warre, with the people and King adjoyning. We exchanged our tinne dish for twentie skinnes, woorth twentie Crownes, or twentie Nobles: and a copper kettle for fiftie skins woorth fifty Crownes. They offered us good exchange for our hatchets, and axes, and for knives, and would have given any thing for swordes: but wee would not depart with any. After two or three dayes the Kings brother came aboord the shippes, and dranke wine, and eat of our meat and of our bread, and liked exceedingly thereof: and after a few dayes overpassed, he brought his wife with him to the ships, his daughter and two or three children: his wife was very well favoured, of meane stature, and very bashfull: shee had on her backe a long cloake of leather, with the furre side next to her body, and before her a piece of the same: about her forehead shee had a bande of white Corall, and so had her husband many times: in her eares shee had bracelets of pearles hanging downe to her middle, (whereof wee delivered your worship a little bracelet) and those were of the bignes of good pease. The rest of her women of the better sort had pendants of copper hanging in either eare, and some of the children of the kings brother and other noble men, have five or sixe in either eare: he himselfe had upon his head a broad plate of golde, or copper, for being unpolished we knew not what mettal it should be, neither would he by any meanes suffer us to take it off his head, but feeling it, it would bow very easily. His apparell was as his wives, onely the women weare their haire long on both sides, and the men but on one. They are of colour yellowish, and their haire black for the most part, and yet we saw children that had very fine aburne, and chestnut coloured haire.

After that these women had bene there, there came downe from all parts great store of people, bringing with them leather, corall, divers kindes of dies very excellent, and exchanged with us: but when Granganimeo the kings brother was present, none durst trade but himselfe: except such as weare red pieces of copper on their heads like himselfe: for that is the difference betweene the noble men, and the governours of countreys, and the meaner sort. And we both noted there, and you have understood since by these men, which we brought home, that no people in the worlde cary more respect to their King, Nobilitie, and Governours, then these doe. The

Kings brothers wife, when she came to us (as she did many times) was followed with forty or fifty women alwayes: and when she came into the shippe, she left them all on land, saving her two daughters, her nurse and one or two more. The Kings brother alwayes kept this order, as many boates as he would come withall to the shippes, so many fires would hee make on the shore a farre off, to the end we might understand with what strength and company he approched. Their boates are made of one tree, either of Pine or of Pitch trees: a wood not commonly knowen to our people, nor found growing in England. They have no edge-tooles to make them withall: if they have any they are very fewe, and those it seemes they had twentie yeres since, which, as those two men declared, was out of a wrake which happened upon their coast of some Christian ship, being beaten that way by some storme and outragious weather, whereof none of the people were saved, but only the ship, or some part of her being cast upon the sand, out of whose sides they drew the nayles and the spikes, and with those they made their best instruments. The manner of making their boates is thus: they burne downe some great tree, or take such as are winde fallen, and putting gumme and rosen upon one side thereof, they set fire into it, and when it hath burnt it hollow, they cut out the coale with their shels, and ever where they would burne it deeper or wider they lay on gummes, which burne away the timber, and by this meanes they fashion very fine boates, and such as will transport twentie men. Their oares are like scoopes, and many times they set with long pooles, as the depth serveth.

The Kings brother had great liking of our armour, a sword, and divers other things which we had: and offered to lay a great boxe of pearle in gage for them: but we refused it for this time, because we would not make them knowe, that we esteemed thereof, untill we had understoode in what places of the countrey the pearle grew: which now your Worshippe doeth very well understand.

THE FIRST VOYAGE TO VIRGINIA

He was very just of his promise: for many times we
delivered him merchandize upon his word, but ever he
came within the day and performed his promise. He
sent us every day a brase or two of fat Bucks, Conies,
Hares, Fish the best of the world. He sent us divers
kindes of fruites, Melons, Walnuts, Cucumbers, Gourdes,
Pease, and divers rootes, and fruites very excellent good,
and of their Countrey corne, which is very white, faire
and well tasted, and groweth three times in five moneths:
in May they sow, in July they reape, in June they sow,
in August they reape: in July they sow, in September
they reape: onely they cast the corne into the ground,
breaking a little of the soft turfe with a wodden mattock,
or pickeaxe: our selves prooved the soile, and put some
of our Pease in the ground, and in tenne dayes they were
of fourteene ynches high: they have also Beanes very
faire of divers colours and wonderfull plentie: some
growing naturally, and some in their gardens, and so
have they both wheat and oates.

The soile is the most plentifull, sweete, fruitfull and
wholsome of all the worlde: there are above foureteene
severall sweete smelling timber trees, and the most part of
their underwoods are Bayes and such like: they have those
Okes that we have, but farre greater and better: After
they had bene divers times aboord our shippes, my selfe,
with seven more went twentie mile into the River, that
runneth towarde the Citie of Skicoak, which River they
call Occam: and the evening following, wee came to an
Island, which they call Raonoak, distant from the harbour
by which we entred, seven leagues: and at the North end
thereof was a village of nine houses, built of Cedar, and
fortified round about with sharpe trees, to keepe out their
enemies, and the entrance into it made like a turne pike
very artificially; when wee came towardes it, standing
neere unto the waters side, the wife of Granganimo the
kings brother came running out to meete us very cheere-
fully and friendly, her husband was not then in the
village; some of her people shee commanded to drawe

our boate on shore for the beating of the billoe: others she appointed to cary us on their backes to the dry ground, and others to bring our oares into the house for feare of stealing. When we were come into the utter roome, having five roomes in her house, she caused us to sit downe by a great fire, and after tooke off our clothes and washed them, and dryed them againe: some of the women plucked off our stockings and washed them, some washed our feete in warme water, and shee her selfe tooke great paines to see all things ordered in the best maner shee could, making great haste to dresse some meate for us to eate.

After we had thus dryed our selves, she brought us into the inner roome, where shee set on the boord standing along the house, some wheate like furmentie, sodden Venison, and roasted, fish sodden, boyled, and roasted, Melons rawe, and sodden, rootes of divers kindes, and divers fruites: their drinke is commonly water, but while the grape lasteth, they drinke wine, and for want of caskes to keepe it, all the yere after they drink water, but it is sodden with Ginger in it, and blacke Sinamon, and sometimes Sassaphras, and divers other wholesome, and medicinable hearbes and trees. We were entertained with all love and kindnesse, and with as much bountie (after their maner) as they could possibly devise. We found the people most gentle, loving, and faithfull, voide of all guile and treason, and such as live after the maner of the golden age. The people onely care howe to defend themselves from the cold in their short winter, and to feed themselves with such meat as the soile affoordeth: there meate is very well sodden and they make broth very sweet and savorie: their vessels are earthen pots, very large, white and sweete, their dishes are wodden platters of sweet timber: within the place where they feede was their lodging, and within that their Idoll, which they worship, of whome they speake incredible things. While we were at meate, there came in at the gates two or three men with their bowes and arrowes from hunting,

whom when wee espied, we beganne to looke one towardes another, and offered to reach our weapons: but
assoone as shee espied our mistrust, shee was very much
mooved, and caused some of her men to runne out, and
take away their bowes and arrowes and breake them, and
withall beate the poore fellowes out of the gate againe.
When we departed in the evening and would not tary all
night, she was very sory, and gave us into our boate our
supper halfe dressed, pottes and all, and brought us to
our boate side, in which wee lay all night, remooving
the same a prettie distance from the shoare: shee perceiving our jelousie, was much greived, and sent divers
men and thirtie women, to sit all night on the banke side
by us, and sent us into our boates five mattes to cover us
from the raine, using very many wordes to intreate us to
rest in their houses: but because wee were fewe men, and
if wee had miscaried, the voyage had bene in very great
danger, wee durst not adventure any thing, though there
was no cause of doubt: for a more kinde and loving
people there can not be found in the worlde, as farre
as we have hitherto had triall.

Beyond this Island there is the maine lande, and over
against this Island falleth into this spacious water, the
great river called Occam by the inhabitants on which
standeth a towne called Pomeiock, & sixe dayes journey
from the same is situate their greatest citie, called Skicoak,
which this people affirme to be very great: but the
Savages were never at it, only they speake of it by the
report of their fathers and other men, whom they have
heard affirme it to bee above one houres journey
about.

Into this river falleth another great river, called Cipo,
in which there is found great store of Muskles in which
there are pearles: likewise there descendeth into this
Occam, another river, called Nomopana, on the one side
whereof standeth a great towne called Chawanook, and
the Lord of that towne and countrey is called Pooneno:
this Pooneno is not subject to the king of Wingandacoa,

A VIRGINIAN PRIEST

but is a free Lord: beyond this country is there another
king, whom they cal Menatonon, and these three kings
are in league with each other. Towards the Southwest,
foure dayes journey is situate a towne called Sequotan,
which is the Southermost towne of Wingandacoa, neere
unto which, sixe and twentie yeres past there was a ship
cast away, whereof some of the people were saved, and
those were white people, whom the countrey people
preserved.

And after ten dayes remaining in an out Island
unhabited, called Wocokon, they with the help of some
of the dwellers of Sequotan, fastened two boates of the
countrey together & made mastes unto them, and sailes of
their shirtes, and having taken into them such victuals as
the countrey yeelded, they departed after they had remained in this out Island 3 weekes: but shortly after it
seemed they were cast away, for the boates were found
upon the coast, cast a land in another Island adjoyning:
other then these, there was never any people apparelled,
or white of colour, either seene or heard of amongst these
people, and these aforesaid were seene onely of the
inhabitantes of Secotan, which appeared to be very true,
for they wondred marvelously when we were amongst
them at the whitenes of our skins, ever coveting to touch
our breasts, and to view the same. Besides they had our
ships in marvelous admiration, & all things els were so
strange unto them, as it appeared that none of them had
ever seene the like. When we discharged any piece,
were it but an hargubuz, they would tremble thereat for
very feare, and for the strangenesse of the same: for the
weapons which themselves use are bowes and arrowes:
the arrowes are but of small canes, headed with a sharpe
shell or tooth of a fish sufficient ynough to kill a naked
man. Their swordes be of wood hardened: likewise they
use wooden breastplates for their defence. They have
besides a kinde of club, in the end whereof they fasten
the sharpe hornes of a stagge, or other beast. When
they goe to warres they cary about with them their idol,

of whom they aske counsel, as the Romans were woont of the Oracle of Apollo. They sing songs as they march towardes the battell in stead of drummes and trumpets: their warres are very cruell and bloody, by reason whereof, and of their civill dissentions which have happened of late yeeres amongst them, the people are marvelously wasted, and in some places the countrey left desolate.

Adjoyning to this countrey aforesaid called Secotan beginneth a countrey called Pomovik, belonging to another king whom they call Piamacum, and this king is in league with the next king adjoyning towards the setting of the Sunne, and the countrey Newsiok, situate upon a goodly river called Neus: these kings have mortall warre with Wingina king of Wingandacoa: but about two yeeres past there was a peace made betweene the King Piemacum, and the Lord of Secotan, as these men which we have brought with us to England, have given us to understand: but there remaineth a mortall malice in the Secotanes, for many injuries & slaughters done upon them by this Piemacum. They invited divers men, and thirtie women of the best of his countrey to their towne to a feast: and when they were altogether merry, & praying before their Idol, (which is nothing els but a meer illusion of the devil) the captaine or Lord of the town came suddenly upon them, and slewe them every one, reserving the women and children: and these two have oftentimes since perswaded us to surprize Piemacum his towne, having promised and assured us, that there will be found in it great store of commodities. But whether their perswasion be to the ende they may be revenged of their enemies, or for the love they beare to us, we leave that to the tryall hereafter.

Beyond this Island called Roanoak, are maine Islands very plentifull of fruits and other naturall increases, together with many townes, and villages, along the side of the continent, some bounding upon the Islands, and some stretching up further into the land.

When we first had sight of this countrey, some thought

the first land we saw to bee the continent: but after we entred into the Haven, we saw before us another mighty long Sea: for there lyeth along the coast a tracte of Islands, two hundreth miles in length, adjoyning to the Ocean sea, and betweene the Islands, two or three entrances: when you are entred betweene them (these Islands being very narrow for the most part, as in most places sixe miles broad, in some places lesse, in fewe more) then there appeareth another great Sea, containing in bredth in some places, forty, and in some fifty, in some twenty miles over, before you come unto the continent: and in this inclosed Sea there are above an hundreth Islands of divers bignesses, whereof one is sixteene miles long, at which we were, finding it a most pleasant and fertile ground, replenished with goodly Cedars, and divers other sweete woods, full of Corrants, of flaxe, and many other notable commodities, which we at that time had no leasure to view. Besides this Island there are many, as I have sayd, some of two, or three, of foure, of five miles, some more, some lesse, most beautifull and pleasant to behold, replenished with Deere, Conies, Hares and divers beasts, and about them the goodliest and best fish in the world, and in greatest abundance.

Thus Sir, we have acquainted you with the particulars of our discovery, made this present voyage, as farre foorth as the shortnesse of the time we there continued would affoord us take viewe of: and so contenting our selves with this service at this time, which wee hope hereafter to inlarge, as occasion and assistance shalbe given, we resolved to leave the countrey, and to apply our selves to returne for England, which we did accordingly, and arrived safely in the West of England about the middest of September.

And whereas wee have above certified you of the countrey taken in possession by us, to her Majesties use, and so to yours by her Majesties grant, wee thought good for the better assurance thereof to record some of the particular Gentlemen, & men of accompt, who then were present, as witnesses of the same, that thereby all occasion of cavill to the title of the countrey, in her Majesties behalfe may be prevented, which otherwise, such as like not the action may use and pretend, whose names are:

Master Philip Amadas,
Master Arthur Barlow,

} Captaines.

William Greenevile,
John Wood,
James Browewich,
Henry Greene,
Benjamin Wood,
Simon Ferdinando,
Nicholas Petman,
John Hewes,

} Of the companie.

We brought home also two of the Savages being lustie men, whose names were Wanchese and Manteo.

SIR WALTER RALEIGH (*ca.* 1552-1618)

VIRGINIA 1584-1607

Notes to Sir Richard Grenville

This first exploratory expedition sent by Ralegh brought back glowing reports of the New World. The corn grew three times in five months and the natives were friendly, as the good fortune of the European sailors, shipwrecked there twenty six years before, demonstrated. There is perhaps always something a little unrealistic about official reports. Certainly Ralegh was told exactly what he wanted to hear but we also know from Thomas Hariot's Report (printed later in this volume) that there were not lacking people willing to spread defamatory stories about the new land and its suitability for settlement. Presumably they, like Ralegh, got their facts from the Barlowe voyage. It is possible, though not certain, that Ralegh got his knighthood for his initiative in organizing this expedition. The Queen graciously accepted Ralegh's well conceived compliment in naming the new land Virginia, but it is interesting to notice the curious similarity of this to the name of the native King Wingina. What the Englishmen took to be the native name of the country, Wingandacoa, was in fact, as Ralegh himself later realised, an Indian phrase meaning "What fine clothes you wear."

Notice too in the Barlowe narrative the picturesquely named Simon Ferdinando. He played a sinister part in the history of the Roanoke colony.

On April 9th, 1585 the first colonists set out from Plymouth under the command of Ralegh's cousin Sir Richard Grenville. Two at least of the settlers were men of considerable distinction—Cavendish the second Englishman to sail right round the globe and Hariot the distinguished mathematician and astronomer.

THE SECOND VOYAGE TO VIRGINIA

The voiage made by Sir Richard Greenvile, for Sir Walter Ralegh, to Virginia, in the yeere 1585.

He 9. day of April, in the yeere abovesayd, we departed from Plymmouth, our Fleete consisting of the number of seven sailes, to wit, the Tyger, of the burden of seven score tunnes, a Flie-boat called the Roe-bucke, of the like burden, the Lyon of a hundred tunnes or thereabouts, the Elizabeth, of fiftie tunnes, and the Dorothie, a small barke: whereunto were also adjoyned for speedy services, two small pinnesses. ⁘ ⁘ ⁘

THE TOWN OF POMEIOCK

we continued our course for Dominica, one of the Antiles of the West India, wherewith we fell the 7. day of May, and the 10. day following wee came to an anker at Cotesa, a little Iland situate neere to the Iland of S. John, where we landed, and refreshed our selves all that day.

The 12. day of May wee came to an anker in the Bay of Moskito, in the Iland of S. John, within a Faulcon shot of the shoare: where our Generall Sir Richard Greenevil, and the most part of our companie landed, and began to fortifie very neere to the Sea side: the river ran by the one side of our forte, and the other two sides were invironed with woods.

The 13. day we began to build a new pinnesse within the Fort, with the timber that wee then felled in the countrey, some part whereof we fet three miles up in the land, and brought it to our Fort upon trucks, the Spaniard not daring to make or offer resistance.

The 16. day there appeared unto us out of the woods eight horsemen of the Spaniards, about a quarter of a mile from our Fort, staying about halfe an houre in viewing our forces: but assoone as they saw ten of our shot marching towards them, they presently retired into the woods.

The 19. day Master Candish, who had bene separated from our fleete in a storme in the Bay of Portugall, arrived at Cotesa, within the sight of the Tiger: we thinking him a farre off to have beene either a Spaniard or Frenchman of warre, thought it good to weigh ankers, and to goe roome with him, which the Tiger did, and discerned him at last to be one of our consorts, for joy of whose comming our ships discharged their ordinance, and saluted him according to the maner of the Seas.

The 22. day twentie other Spanish horsemen shewed themselves to us upon the other side of the river: who being seene, our Generall dispatched 20. footemen towards them, and two horsmen of ours, mounted upon Spanish horses, which wee before had taken in the time of our being on the Iland: they shewed to our men a flagge of truce, and made signes to have a parle with us: whereupon two of our men' went halfe of the way upon the sands, and two of theirs came and met them: the two Spaniards offered very great salutations to our men, but began according to their Spanish proud humors, to expostulate with them about their arrivall and fortifying in their countrey, who notwithstanding by our mens discreet answers were so cooled, that (whereas they were told, that our principall intention was onely to furnish our selves with water and victuales, and other necessaries, wherof we stood in neede, which we craved might be yeelded us with faire and friendly meanes, otherwise our resolution was to practise force, and to relieve ourselves by the sworde) the Spaniards in conclusion seeing our men so resolute, yeelded to our requestes with large promises of all curtesie, and great favour, and so our men and theirs departed.

The 23. day our pinnesse was finished, and lanched: which being done, our Generall with his Captaines and Gentlemen, marched up into the Countrey about the space of 4. miles, where in a plaine marsh they stayed expecting the comming of the Spaniards according to their promise, to furnish us with victuals: who keeping their olde custome for perjurie and breach of promise, came not, whereupon our Generall fired the woods thereabout, and so retired to our Fort, which the same day was fired also, and each man came aboord to be ready to set saile the next morning.

The 29. day wee set saile from Saint Johns, being many of us stung before upon shoare with the Muskitos: but the same night wee tooke a Spanish Frigat, which was forsaken by the Spaniards upon the sight of us, and the next day in the morning very early we tooke another Frigat, with good and rich fraight, and divers Spaniards of account in her, which afterwards wee ransomed for good round summes, and landed them in S. Johns.

The 26. day our Lieutenant Master Ralph Lane went in one of the Frigats which we had taken, to Roxo bay upon the Southwest side of Saint Johns, to fetch salt, being thither conducted by a Spanish Pilot: as soone as hee arrived there, hee landed with his men to the number of 20. and intrenched himselfe upon the sandes immediatly, compassing one of their salte hils within the trench: who being seene of the Spaniards, there came downe towardes him two or three troopes of horsemen and footmen, who gave him the looking, and gazing on, but durst not come neere him to offer any resistance, so that Master Lane maugre their troopes, caryed their salte aboord and laded his Frigat, and so returned againe to our fleete the 29. day, which road at S. Germans Bay. The same day we all departed, and the next day arrived in the Iland of Hispaniola.

June.

THe 1. day of June we anchored at Isabella, on the North side of Hispaniola.

The 3. day of June, the Governour of Isabella, and Captaine of the Port de Plata, being certified by the reports of sundry Spaniards, who had beene well intertained aboord our shippes by our Generall, that in our fleete were many brave and gallant Gentlemen, who greatly desired to see the Governour aforesayd, he thereupon sent gentle commendations to our Generall, promising within few dayes to come to him in person, which he perfourmed accordingly.

The 5. day the aforesayd Governour accompanied with a lusty Fryer, and twenty other Spaniards, with their servants, and Negroes, came downe to the Sea side, where our ships road at anker, who being seene, our Generall manned immediatly the most part of his boates with the chiefe men of our Fleete, every man appointed, and furnished in the best sort: at the landing of our Generall, the Spanish governour received him very courteously, and the Spanish Gentlemen saluted our English Gentlemen, and their inferiour sort did also salute our Souldiers and Sea men, liking our men, and likewise their qualities, although at the first they seemed to stand in feare of us, and of so many of our boates, whereof they desired that all might not land their men, yet in the end, the courtesies that passed on both sides were so great, that all feare and mistrust on the Spaniards part was abandoned.

In the meane time while our English Generall and the Spanish Governour discoursed betwixt them of divers matters, as of the state of the Countrey, the multitude of the Townes and people, and the commodities of the Iland, our men provided two banquetting houses covered with greene boughes, the one for the Gentlemen, the other for the servaunts, and a sumptuous banquet was brought in served by us all in plate, with the sound of trumpets, and consort of musicke, wherwith the Spaniards were more then delighted. Which banquet being ended, the Spaniardes in recompence of our courtesie, caused a great heard of white buls, and kyne to be brought together from the mountaines, and appoynted for every Gentleman and Captaine that would ride, a horse ready sadled, and then singled out three of the best of them to bee hunted by horsemen after their maner, so that the pastime grewe very pleasant for the space of three houres, wherein all three of the beasts were killed, whereof one tooke the Sea, and there was slaine with a musket. After this sport, many rare presents and gifts were given and bestowed on both parts, and the next day wee played the Marchants in bargaining with them by way of trucke and exchange of divers of their commodities, as horses, mares, kine, buls, goates, swine, sheepe, bull-hides, sugar, ginger, pearle, tabacco, and such like commodities of the Iland.

The 7. day we departed with great good will from the Spaniards from the Iland of Hispaniola: but the wiser sort doe impute this great shew of friendship, and courtesie used towards us by the Spaniards rather to the force that wee were of, and the vigilancie, and watchfulnesse that was amongst us, then to any heartie good will, or sure friendly intertainement: for doubtlesse if they had bene stronger then wee, wee might have looked for no better curtesie at their handes, then Master John Haukins received at Saint John de Ullua, or John Oxnam neere the streights of Dariene, and divers others of our Countrymen in other places.

The 8. day we ankred at a small Iland to take Seales, which in that place wee understood to have bene in great quantitie, where the Generall and certaine others with him in the pinnesse were in very great danger to have beene all cast away, but by the helpe of God they escaped the hasard, and returned aboord the Admirall in safetie.

The 12. we ankered at Guanima, and landed.

The 15. and 16. we ankered and landed at Cyguateo.

The 20. we fell with the maine of Florida.

The 23. we were in great danger of a wracke on a breach called the Cape of Feare.

The 24. we came to anker in a harbour, where wee caught in one tyde so much fish as would have yeelded us twentie pounds in London: this was our first landing in Florida.

The 26. we came to anker at Wocokon.

The 29. wee weighed anker to bring the Tyger into the harbour, where through the unskilfulnesse of the Master whose name was Fernando, the Admirall strooke on ground, and sunke.....

Julie.

The 3. we sent word of our arriving at Wococon, to Wingina at Roanoak.

The 6. M. John Arundel was sent to the maine, and Manteo with him: and Captaine Aubry and Captaine Boniten the same day were sent to Croatoan, where they found two of our men left there with 30. other by Captaine Reymond, some 20. dayes before.

The 8. Captaine Aubry and Captaine Boniten returned, with two of our men found by them, to us at Wocokon.

The 11. day the Generall accompanied in his Tilt boate with Master John Arundell, Master Stukeley, and divers other Gentlemen, Master Lane, Master Candish, Master Hariot, and twentie others in the new pinnesse, Captaine Amadas, Captaine Clarke, with ten others in a shipboat, Francis Brooke, and John White in another ship-boate, passed over the water from Wococon to the maine land victualled for eight dayes, in which voyage we first discovered the townes of Pomejok, Aquascogoc and Secotan, and also the great lake called by the Savages Paquipe, with divers other places, and so returned with that discovery to our Fleete.

The 12. we came to the Towne of Pomeiok.

The 13. we passed by water to Aquascogok.

The 15. we came to Secotan, and were well entertained there of the Savages.

The 16. wee returned thence, and one of our boates with the Admirall was sent to Aquascogok, to demaund a silver cup which one of the Savages had stollen from us, and not receiving it according to his promise, wee burnt, and spoyled their corne, and Towne, all the people being fled.

The 18. we returned from the discovery of Secotan, and the same day came aboord our Fleete ryding at Wococon.

The 21. our Fleete ankering at Wococon, we wayed anker for Hatoraske.

The 27. our Fleete ankered at Hatorask, and there we rested.

The 29. Grangino brother to king Wingina came aboord the Admirall, and Manteo with him.

The 2. the Admirall was sent to Weapomeiok.

The 5. M. John Arundell was sent for England.

THE SECOND VOYAGE TO VIRGINIA

The 25. our Generall wayed anker, and set saile for England.

About the 31. he tooke a Spanish ship of 300 tunne richly loaden, boording her with a boate made with boards of chests, which fell asunder, and sunke at the ships side, assoone as ever he and his men were out of it.

The 10. of September, by foule weather the Generall then shipped in the prize, lost sight of the Tyger.

The 6. the Tyger fell with the Landes end, and the same day came to anker at Falmouth.

The 18. the General came with the prize to Plymmouth, and was courteously received by divers of his worshipfull friends.

The names of those as well Gentlemen as others, that remained one whole yeere in Virginia, under the Governement of Master Ralph Lane.

MAster Philip Amadas, Admirall of the countrey.
Master Hariot.
Master Acton.
Master Edward Stafford.
Thomas Luddington.
Master Marvyn.
Master Gardiner.
Captaine Vaughan.
Master Kendall.
Master Prideox.
Robert Holecroft.
Rise Courtney.
Master Hugh Rogers.
Master Thomas Harvie.
Master Snelling.
Master Anthony Russe.

Richard Gilbert.
Steven Pomarie.
John Brocke.
Bennet Harrie.
James Stevenson.
Charles Stevenson.
Christopher Lowde.
Jeremie Man.
James Mason.
David Salter.
Richard Ireland.
Thomas Bookener.
William Philips.
Randall Mayne.
James Skinner.
George Eseven.
John Chandeler.
Philip Blunt.

With divers others to the number of 108.

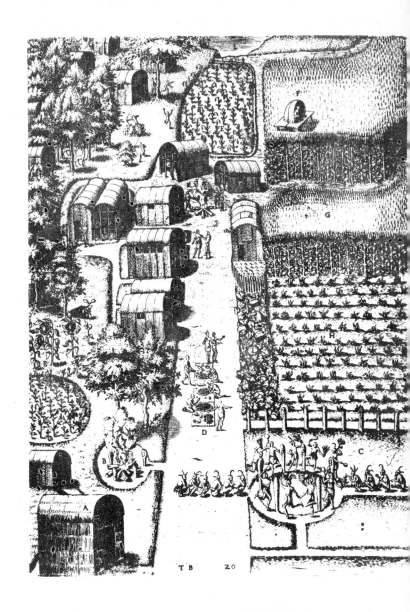

THE VILLAGE OF SECOTON

An extract of Master Ralph Lanes letter to M. Richard Hakluyt Esquire, and another Gentleman of the middle Temple, from Virginia.

N the meane while you shall understand, that since Sir Richard Greenvils departure from us, as also before, we have discovered the maine to be the goodliest oyle under the cope of heaven, so abounding with sweete trees, that bring such sundry rich and pleasant gummes, grapes of such greatnesse, yet wilde, as France, Spaine nor Italie have no greater, so many sorts of Apothecarie drugs, such severall kindes of flaxe, & one kind like silke, the same gathered of a grasse, as common there, as grasse is here. And now within these few dayes we have found here Maiz or Guinie wheate, whose eare yeeldeth corne for bread 400. upon one eare, and the Cane maketh very good and perfect sugar, also Terra Samia, otherwise Terra sigillata. Besides that, it is the goodliest and most pleasing Territorie of the world: for the continent is of an huge and unknowen greatnesse, and very well peopled and towned, though savagely, and the climate so wholsome, that wee had not one sicke since we touched the land here. To conclude, if Virginia had but horses and kine in some reasonable proportion, I dare assure my selfe being inhabited with English, no realme in Christendome were comparable to it. For this already we finde, that what commodities soever Spaine, France, Italy, or the East partes doe yeeld unto us, in wines of all sortes, in oyles, in flaxe, in rosens, pitch, frankensence, corrans, sugers, and such like, these parts doe abound with the growth of them all, but being Savages that possesse the land, they know no use of the same. And sundry other rich commodities, that no parts of the world, be they West or East Indies, have, here wee finde great abundance of. The people naturally are most

courteous, and very desirous to have clothes, but especially of course cloth rather then silke, course canvas they also like well of, but copper caryeth the price of all, so it be made red. Thus good M. Hakluyt and M. H. I have joyned you both in one letter of remembrance, as two that I love dearely well, and commending me most heartily to you both, I commit you to the tuition of the Almightie. From the new Fort in Virginia, this third of September, 1585.

Your most assured friend RALPH LANE.

An account of the particularities of the imployments of the English men left in Virginia by Sir Richard Greenevill under the charge of Master Ralph Lane Generall of the same, from the 17. of August 1585. until the 18. of June 1586. at which time they departed the Countrey: sent and directed to Sir Walter Ralegh.

Hat I may proceede with order in this discourse, I thinke it requisite to divide it into two parts. The first shall declare the particularities of such parts of the Countrey within the maine, as our weake number, and supply of things necessarie did inable us to enter into the discovery of.

The second part shall set downe the reasons generally moving us to resolve on our departure at the instant with the Generall Sir Francis Drake, and our common request for passage with him, when the barkes, pinnesses, and boates with the Masters and Mariners meant by him to bee left in the Countrey, for the supply of such, as for a further time meant to have stayed there, were caryed away with tempest and foule weather: In the beginning whereof shall bee declared the conspiracie of Pemisapan, with the Savages of the maine to have cut us off, &c.

RALPH LANE

Notes to Ralph Lane's Report

The colony stayed in Virginia from August 17th, 1585 to June 18th, 1586 when they took passage back to England with Sir Francis Drake. The Governor of the colony was another Devon man, Ralph Lane. Here is his own account of what befell them.

The second part touching the conspiracie of Pemisapan, the discovery of the same, and at the last, of our request to depart with Sir Francis Drake for England.

The first part of the report is here omitted. It tells of Ralph Lane's expeditions in quest of food and the difficulties and dangers he encounters.

Ensenore, king Wingina's father, had died on 20th April 1586. With him the colonists had lost their only faithful friend among the savages. Wingina, who after the death of his brother Granganimo has assumed the name of Pemisapan, plans a conspiracy to wipe out the colony. This is his plan:

First that Okisko king of Weopomeiok with the Mandoages should bee mooved, and with great quantitie of copper intertained to the number of 7. or 8. hundreth bowes, to enterprise the matter thus to be ordered. They of Weopomeiok should be invited to a certaine kind of moneths minde which they doe use to solemnise in their Savage maner for any great personage dead, and should have bene for Ensenore. At this instant also should the Mandoaks, who were a great people, with the Chesepians & their friends to the number of 700. of them, be armed at a day appointed to the maine of Dasamonquepeio, and there lying close at the signe of fiers, which should interchangeably be made on both sides, when Pemisapan with his troupe above named should have executed me, and some of our Weroances (as they called all our principall officers,) the maine forces of the rest should have come over into the Iland, where they ment to have dispatched the rest of the company, whom they did imagine to finde both dismayed and dispersed abroad in the Island, seeking of crabs and fish to live withall. The maner of their enterprise was this.

Tarraquine and Andacon two principall men about
Pemisapan, and very lustie fellowes, with twentie more
appointed to them had the charge of my person to see an
order taken for the same, which they ment should in this
sort have been executed. In the dead time of the night
they would have beset my house, and put fire in the
reedes that the same was covered with: meaning (as it
was likely) that my selfe would have come running out
of a sudden amazed in my shirt without armes, upon the
instant whereof they would have knocked out my braines.

The same order was given to certaine of his fellowes,
for M. Heriots: so for all the rest of our better sort, all
our houses at one instant being set on fire as afore is
saide, and that as well for them of the fort, as for us at
the towne. Now to the ende that we might be the
fewer in number together, and so bee the more easily
dealt withall (for in deed tenne of us with our armes
prepared, were a terrour to a hundred of the best sort of
them,) they agreed and did immediatly put it in practise,
that they should not for any copper sell us any victuals
whatsoever: besides that in the night they should sende
to have our weares robbed, and also to cause them to bee
broken, and once being broken never to be repaired
againe by them. By this meanes the King stood assured,
that I must bee enforced for lacke of sustenance there, to
disband my company into sundry places to live upon
shell fish, for so the Savages themselves doe, going to
Hatorask, Croatoan, and other places, fishing and hunting,
while their grounds be in sowing, and their corne growing: which failed not his expectation. For the famine
grew so extreme among us, or weares failing us of fish,
that I was enforced to sende Captaine Stafford with 20.
with him to Croatoan my Lord Admirals Iland to serve
two turnes in one, that is to say, to feede himselfe and
his company, and also to keepe watch if any shipping
came upon the coast to warne us of the same. I sent M.
Pridiox with the pinnesse to Hatorask, and ten with him,
with the Provost Marshal to live there, and also to wait

for shipping: also I sent every weeke 16. or 20. of the rest of the company to the maine over against us, to live of Casada and oysters.

In the meane while Pemisapan went of purpose to Dasamonquepeio for three causes: The one to see his grounds there broken up, and sowed for a second crop: the other to withdrawe himselfe from my dayly sending to him for supply of victuall for my company, for hee was afraid to deny me any thing, neither durst hee in my presence but by colour and with excuses, which I was content to accept for the time, meaning in the ende as I had reason, to give him the jumpe once for all: but in the meane whiles, as I had ever done before, I and mine bare all wrongs, and accepted of all excuses.

My purpose was to have relied my selfe with Mena-tonon, and the Chaonists, who in trueth as they are more valiant people and in greater number then the rest, so are they more faithfull in their promises, and since my late being there had given many tokens of earnest desire they had to joyne in perfect league with us, and therefore were greatly offended with Pemisapan and Weopomeiok for making him beleeve such tales of us.

The third cause of this going to Dasamonquepeio was to dispatch his messengers to Weopomeiok, and to the Mandoages as aforesaid: all which he did with great imprest of copper in hand, making large promises to them of greater spoile.

The answere within few dayes after came from Weo-pomeiok, which was devided into two parts. First for the King Okisko, who denied to be of the partie for him-selfe, or any of his especiall followers, and therefore did immediatly retire himselfe with his force into the maine: the other was concerning the rest of the said province who accepted of it: and in like sort the Mandoags received the imprest.

The day of their assembly aforesaid at Roanoak was appointed the 10. of June: all which the premises were discovered by Skyco, the King Menatonon his sonne my

E

prisoner, who having once attempted to run away, I laid him in the bylboes, threatning to cut off his head, whom I remitted at Pemisapans request : whereupon hee being perswaded that hee was our enemie to the death, he did not onely feed him with himselfe, but also made him acquainted with all his practises. On the other side, the yong man finding himselfe as well used at my hande, as I had meanes to shew, and that all my company made much of him, he flatly discovered al unto me, which also afterwards was reveiled unto me by one of Pemisapans owne men, that night before he was slaine.

These mischiefes being all instantly upon me and my company to be put in execution, it stood mee in hand to study how to prevent them, and also to save all others, which were at that time as aforesaid so farre from me: whereupon I sent to Pemisapan to put suspition out of his head, that I meant presently to go to Croatoan, for that I had heard of the arrivall of our fleete, (though I in trueth had neither heard nor hoped for so good adventure,) and that I meant to come by him, to borrow of his men to fish for my company, & to hunt for me at Croatoan, as also to buy some foure dayes provision to serve for my voyage.

He sent me word that he would himselfe come over to Roanoak, but from day to day he deferred, onely to bring the Weopomeioks with him & the Mandoags, whose time appointed was within eight dayes after. It was the last of May 1586 when all his owne Savages began to make their assembly at Roanoak, at his commandement sent abroad unto them, and I resolved not to stay longer upon his comming over, since he meant to come with so good company, but thought good to go and visit him with such as I had, which I resolved to do the next day : but that night I meant by the way to give them in the Island a canvisado, and at the instant to seize upon all the canoas about the Island, to keepe him from advertisements.

But the towne tooke the alarme before I meant it to

them: the occasion was this. I had sent the Master of the light horseman, with a few with him, to gather up all the canoas in the setting of the Sun, & to take as many as were going from us to Dasamonquepeio, but to suffer any that came from thence, to land. He met with a Canoa going from the shore, and overthrew the Canoa, and cut off two Savages heads: this was not done so secretly but he was discovered from the shore; wherupon the cry arose: for in trueth they, privy to their owne villanous purposes against us, held as good espiall upon us, both day and night, as we did upon them.

The allarme given, they tooke themselves to their bowes, and we to our armes: some three or foure of them at the first were slaine with our shot: the rest fled into the woods. The next morning with the light horsman & one Canoa taking 25 with the Colonel of the Chesepians, and the Sergeant major, I went to Dasamonquepeio: and being landed, sent Pemisapan word by one of his owne Savages that met me at the shore, that I was going to Croatoan, and meant to take him in the way to complaine unto him of Osocon, who the night past was conveying away my prisoner, whom I had there present tied in an handlocke. Heere-upon the king did abide my comming to him, and find-ing my selfe amidst seven or eight of his principall Weroances and followers, (not regarding any of the common sort) I gave the watch-word agreed upon, (which was, Christ our victory) and immediatly those his chiefe men and himselfe had by the mercy of God for our deliverance, that which they had purposed for us. The king himselfe being shot thorow by the Colonell with a pistoll, lying on the ground for dead, & I looking as watchfully for the saving of Manteos friends, as others were busie that none of the rest should escape, suddenly he started up, and ran away as though he had not bene touched, insomuch as he overran all the company, being by the way shot thwart the buttocks by mine Irish boy with my petronell. In the end an

Irish man serving me, one Nugent, and the deputy provost, undertooke him; and following him in the woods, overtooke him: and I in some doubt least we had lost both the king & my man by our owne negligence to have beene intercepted by the Savages, wee met him returning out of the woods with Pemisapans head in his hand.

This fell out the first of June 1586, and the eight of the same came advertisement to me from captaine Stafford, lying at my lord Admirals Island, that he had discovered a great fleet of three and twenty sailes: but whether they were friends or foes, he could not yet discerne. He advised me to stand upon as good guard as I could.

The ninth of the sayd moneth he himselfe came unto me, having that night before, & that same day travelled by land twenty miles: and I must truely report of him from the first to the last; hee was the gentleman that never spared labour or perill either by land or water, faire weather or foule, to performe any service committed unto him.

He brought me a letter from the Generall Sir Francis Drake, with a most bountifull and honourable offer for the supply of our necessities to the performance of the action wee were entred into; and that not only of victuals, munition, and clothing, but also of barks, pinnesses, and boats; they also by him to be victualled, manned, and furnished to my contentation.

The tenth day he arrived in the road of our bad harborow: and comming there to an anker, the eleventh day I came to him, whom I found in deeds most honourably to performe that which in writing and message he had most curteously offered, he having aforehand propounded the matter to all the captaines of his fleet, and got their liking and consent thereto.

With such thanks unto him and his captaines for his care both of us and of our action, not as the matter deserved, but as I could both for my company and my selfe, I (being aforehand prepared what I would desire) craved at his hands that it would please him to take with him into England a number of weake and unfit men for my good action, which I would deliver to him; and in place of them to supply me of his company with oare-men, artificers, and others.

That he would leave us so much shipping and victuall, as about August then next following would cary me and all my company into England, when we had discovered somewhat, that for lacke of needfull provision in time left with us as yet remained undone.

That it woulde please him withall to leave some sufficient Masters not onely to cary us into England, when time should be, but also to search the coast for some better harborow, if there were any, and especially to helpe us to some small boats and oare-men.

Also for a supply of calievers, hand weapons, match and lead, tooles, apparell, and such like.

He having received these my requests, according to his usuall commendable maner of government (as it was told me) calling his captaines to counsell; the resolution was that I should send such of my officers of my company as I used in such matters, with their notes, to goe aboord with him; which were the Master of the victuals, The Keeper of the store, and the Vicetreasurer: to whom he appointed forthwith for me The Francis, being a very proper barke of 70 tun, and tooke present order for bringing of victual aboord her for 100 men for foure moneths, with all my other demands whatsoever, to the uttermost.

And further, he appointed for me two pinnesses, and foure small boats: and that which was to performe all his former liberality towards us, was that he had gotten the full assents of two of as sufficient experimented Masters as were any in his fleet, by judgement of them that knew them, with very sufficient gings to tary with me, and to imploy themselves most earnestly in the action, as I should appoint them, untill the terme which

I promised of our returne into England againe. The
names of one of those Masters was Abraham Kendall,
the other Griffith Herne.

While these things were in hand, the provision aforesayd being brought, and in bringing aboord, my sayd
Masters being also gone aboord, my sayd barks having
accepted of their charge, and mine owne officers, with
others in like sort of my company with them (all which
was dispatched by the sayd Generall the 12 of the sayde
moneth) the 13 of the same there arose such an un-
woonted storme, and continued foure dayes, that had
like to have driven all on shore, if the Lord had not
held his holy hand over them, and the Generall very
providently foreseene the woorst himselfe, then about
my dispatch putting himselfe aboord: but in the end
having driven sundry of the fleet to put to Sea the
Francis also with all my provisions, my two Masters,
and my company aboord, she was seene to be free from
the same, and to put cleere to Sea.

This storme having continued from the 13 to the 16
of the moneth, and thus my barke put away as aforesayd, the Generall comming ashore made a new proffer
unto me; which was a ship of 170 tunne, called The
Barke Bonner, with a sufficient Master and guide to
tary with me the time appointed, and victualled sufficiently to cary me and my company into England, with
all provisions as before: but he tolde me that he would
not for any thing undertake to have her brought into
our harbour, and therefore he was to leave her in the
road, and to leave the care of the rest unto my selfe,
and advised me to consider with my company of our
case, and to deliver presently unto him in writing what
I would require him to doe for us: which being within
his power, he did assure me aswell for his Captaines as
for himselfe, should be most willingly performed.

Heereupon calling such Captaines and gentlemen of
my company as then were at hand, who were all as
privy as my selfe to the Generals offer: their whole re-

quest was to me, that considering the case that we stood in, the weaknesse of our company, the small number of the same, the carying away of our first appointed barke, with those two especiall Masters, with our principall provisions in the same, by the very hand of God as it seemed, stretched out to take us from thence; considering also, that his second offer, though most honourable of his part, yet of ours not to be taken, insomuch as there was no possibility for her with any safety to be brought into the harbour: seeing furthermore, our hope for supply with Sir Richard Greenvill, so undoubtedly promised us before Easter, not yet come, neither then likely to come this yeere, considering the doings in England for Flanders, and also for America, that therefore I would resolve my selfe with my company to goe into England in that fleet, and accordingly to make request to the Generall in all our names, that he would be pleased to give us present passage with him. Which request of ours by my selfe delivered unto him, hee most readily assented unto: and so he sending immediatly his pinnesses unto our Island for the fetching away of a few that there were left with our baggage, the weather was so boisterous, & the pinnesses so often on ground, that the most of all we had, with all our Cards, Books and writings were by the Sailers cast overboord, the greater number of the fleet being much agrieved with their long and dangerous abode in that miserable road.

From whence the Generall in the name of the Almighty, weying his ankers (having bestowed us among his fleet) for the reliefe of whom hee had in that storme susteined more perill of wracke then in all his former most honourable actions against the Spanyards, with praises unto God for all, set saile the nineteenth of June 1586, and arrived in Portsmouth the seven and twentieth of July the same yeere.

HOW THEY COOK

HOW THEY EAT

40

Mil.aur.

GRENVILVS RICHARDVS

Notes to Sir Richard Grenville

Ralph Lane's colonists had been 'too quick despairers', for a day or two after Drake had sailed with them aboard the relief ships promised by Ralegh arrived. They searched in vain for the settlers and when, a fortnight later, Grenville himself appeared he had to decide what his proper course of action should be. Leaving with them stores for two years, he planted a tiny garrison of fifteen men to hold the land for England and set off for home. An anonymous report on Grenville's relief expedition gives us the full story.

41

The third voyage made by a ship sent in the yeere 1586, to the reliefe of the Colony planted in Virginia, at the sole charges of Sir Walter Ralegh.

N the yeere of our Lord 1586 Sir Walter Ralegh at his owne charge prepared a ship of an hundred tunne, fraighted with all maner of things in most plentifull maner, for the supply and reliefe of his Colony then remaining in Virginia: but before they set saile from England it was after Easter, so that our Colony halfe despaired of the comming of any supply: wherefore every man prepared for himselfe, determining resolutely to spend the residue of their life time in that countrey. And for the better performance of this their determination, they sowed, planted, and set such things as were necessary for their reliefe in so plentifull a maner as might have sufficed them two yeeres without any further labour. Thus trusting to their owne harvest, they passed the Summer till the tenth of June: at which time their corne which they had sowed was within one fortnight of reaping: but then it happened that Sir Francis Drake in his prosperous returne from the sacking of Sant Domingo, Cartagena, and Saint Augustine, determined in his way homeward to visit his countreymen the English Colony then remaining in Virginia. So passing along the coasts of Florida, he fell with the parts where our English Colony inhabited: and having espied some of that company, there he ankered and went aland, where hee conferred with them of their state and welfare, and how things had past with them. They answered him that they lived all; but hitherto in some scarsity: and as yet could heare of no supply out of England: therefore they requested him that hee would leave with them some two or three ships, that if in some reasonable time they heard not out of

England, they might then returne themselves. Which hee agreed to. Whilest some were then writing their letters to send into England, and some others making reports of the accidents of their travels ech to other, some on land, some on boord, a great storme arose, and drove the most of their fleet from their ankers to Sea, in which ships at that instant were the chiefest of the English Colony: the rest on land perceiving this, hasted to those three sailes which were appointed to be left there; and for feare they should be left behinde they left all things confusedly, as if they had bene chased from thence by a mighty army: and no doubt so they were; for the hand of God came upon them for the cruelty and outrages committed by some of them against the native inhabitants of that countrey.

Immediatly after the departing of our English Colony out of this paradise of the world, the ship abovementioned sent and set forth at the charges of Sir Walter Ralegh and his direction, arrived at Hatorask; who after some time spent in seeking our Colony up in the countrey, and not finding them, returned with all the aforesayd provision into England.

About foureteene or fifteene dayes after the departure of the aforesayd shippe, Sir Richard Grinvile Generall of Virginia, accompanied with three shippes well appointed for the same voyage, arrived there; who not finding the aforesayd shippe according to his expectation, nor hearing any newes of our English Colony there seated, and left by him anno 1585, himselfe travelling up into divers places of the countrey, aswell to see if he could heare any newes of the Colony left there by him the yeere before, under the charge of Master Lane his deputy, as also to discover some places of the countrey: but after some time spent therein, not hearing any newes of them, and finding the places which they inhabited desolate, yet unwilling to loose the possession of the countrey which Englishmen had so long held: after good deliberation, hee determined to leave some men behinde to reteine

possession of the Countrey: whereupon he landed
fifteene men in the Isle of Roanoak, furnished plentifully
with all maner of provision for two yeeres, and so
departed for England.

Not long after he fell with the Isles of Açores, on some
of which Islands he landed, and spoiled the townes of all
such things as were woorth cariage, where also he tooke
divers Spanyards. With these and many other exploits
done by him in this voyage, aswell outward as homeward,
he returned into England.

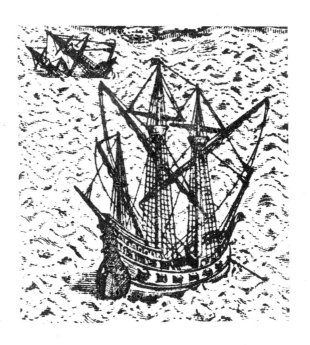

PRAYING AROUND THE FIRE

CHIEFTAIN OF VIRGINIA

AN OLD MAN IN HIS WINTER CLOTHES

A briefe and true report
of the new found land of Virginia.
of the commodities and of the nature and man
ners of the naturall inhabitants. Diſcouered by
the Engliſh Colony there ſeated by Sir Richard
Greinuile Knight In the yeere 1585. Which Rema
: ined Vnder the gouernement of twelue monethes,
At the ſpeciall charge and direction of the Honourable SIR WALTER RALEIGH Knight lord Warden
of the ſtanneries Who therein hath beene fauoured
and authoriſed by her MAIESTIE
and her letters patents:
This fore booke Is made in Engliſh
BY Thomas Hariot ſeruant to the abouenamed
Sir WALTER, a member of the Colony, and there
imployed in diſcouering

CVM GRATIA ET PRIVILEGIO CÆS MA^{TIS} SPECIA^{LE}

FRANCOFORTI AD MOENVM
TIPIS IOANNIS WECHELI, SVMTIBVS VERO THEODORI
DE BRY ANNO CD D XC.
VENALES REPERIVNTVR IN OFFICINA SIGISMVNDI FEIRABENDII

Hariot's *Briefe and True Report*, published
by Theodore De Bry in 1590.

47

HOW THEY CATCH FISH

An extract of

A briefe and true report of the new found land
of Virginia: of the commodities there found,
and to be raised, aswell merchantable as others:
Written by Thomas Heriot, servant to Sir
Walter Ralegh, a member of the Colony,
and there imployed in discovering a full
twelvemoneth.

Rafe Lane one of her Majesties Esquiers, and
Governour of the Colony in Virginia, above
mentioned, for the time there resident, to the
gentle Reader wisheth all happinesse in the
Lord.

Lbeit (gentle Reader) the credit of the
reports in this Treatise contained can
little be furthered by the testimony of
one as my selfe, through affection judged
partiall, though without desert: neverthelesse, forsomuch as I have bene requested
by some my particular friends, who
conceive more rightly of me, to deliver freely my
knowledge of the same, not onely for the satisfying
of them, but also for the true information of any other
whosoever, that comes not with a prejudicate minde
to the reading thereof: thus much upon my credit I am
to affirme, that things universally are so truely set downe

in this Treatise by the authour thereof, an actor in the Colony, and a man no lesse for his honesty then learning commendable, as that I dare boldly avouch, it may very well passe with the credit of trueth even amongst the most true relations of this age. Which as for mine owne part I am ready any way with my word to acknowledge, so also (of the certaintie thereof assured by mine owne experience) with this my publique assertion I doe affirme the same. Farewell in the Lord.

To the Adventurers, Favourers, and Welwillers of the enterprise for the inhabiting and planting in Virginia.

Ince the first undertaking by Sir Walter Ralegh to deale in the action of discovering of that countrey which is now called and knowen by the name of Virginia, many voyages having beene thither made at sundry times to his great charge; as first in the yere 1584, and afterwards in the yeres 1585, 1586, and now of late this last yeere 1587: there have bene divers and variable reports, with some slanderous and shamefull speeches bruted abroad by many that returned from thence: especially of that discovery which was made by the Colony transported by Sir Richard Grinvile in the yere 1585, being of all others the most principall, and as yet of most effect, the time of their abode in the countrey being a whole yere, when as in the other voyage before they stayed but sixe weeks, and the others after were onely for supply and transportation, nothing more being discovered then had bene before. Which reports have not done a little wrong to many that otherwise would have also favoured and adventured in the action, to the honour and benefit of our nation, besides the particular profit and credit which would redound to themselves the dealers therein, as I hope by the sequel of events, to the shame of those that have avouched the contrary, shall be manifest, if you the adventurers, favourers and welwillers doe but either increase in number, or in opinion continue, or having beene doubtfull, renew your good liking and furtherance to deale therein according to the woorthinesse thereof already found, and as you shall understand hereafter to be requisit. Touching which woorthinesse through cause of the diversity of relations and reports, many of your opinions could not be firme, nor the minds of some that are well disposed be setled in any certaintie.

I have therefore thought it good, being one that have beene in the discoverie, and in dealing with the naturall inhabitants specially imployed: and having therefore seene and knowen more then the ordinary, to impart so much unto you of the fruits of our labours, as that you may know how injuriously the enterprise is slandered, and that in publique maner at this present, chiefly for two respects.

First, that some of you which are yet ignorant or doubtfull of the state thereof, may see that there is sufficient cause why the chiefe enterpriser with the favour of her Majesty, notwithstanding such reports, hath not onely since continued the action by sending into the countrey againe, and replanting this last yeere a new Colony, but is also ready, according as the times and meanes will affoord, to follow and prosecute the same.

Secondly, that you seeing and knowing the continuance of the action, by the view hereof you may generally know and learne what the countrey is, and thereupon consider how your dealing therein, if it proceed, may returne you profit and gaine, be it either by inhabiting and planting, or otherwise in furthering thereof.

And least that the substance of my relation should be doubtfull unto you, as of others by reason of their diversitie, I will first open the cause in a few words, wherefore they are so different, referring my selfe to

THE MARKS OF THE CHIEF MEN OF VIRGINIA

HOW THEY BOIL MEAT

your favourable constructions, and to be adjudged of,
as by good consideration you shall finde cause.

Of our company that returned, some for their mis-
demeanour and ill dealing in the countrey have bene
there worthily punished, who by reason of their bad
natures, have maliciously not onely spoken ill of their
Governours, but for their sakes slandered the countrey
it selfe. The like also have those done which were of
their consort.

Some being ignorant of the state thereof, notwithstanding since their returne amongst their friends &
acquaintance, and also others, especially if they were in
company where they might not be gainsayd, would
seeme to know so much as no men more, and make
no men so great travellers as themselves. They stood
so much, as it may seeme, upon their credit and reputation, that having bene a twelvemoneth in the
countrey, it would have bene a great disgrace unto
them, as they thought, if they could not have sayd
much, whether it were true or false. Of which some
have spoken of more then ever they saw, or otherwise
knew to be there. Other some have not bene ashamed
to make absolute deniall of that, which although not
by them, yet by others is most certainly and there
plentifully knowen, & other some make difficulties of
those things they have no skill of.

The cause of their ignorance was, in that they were
of that many that were never out of the Island where
we were seated, or not farre, or at the least wise in
few places els, during the time of our abode in the
country: or of that many, that after gold & silver was
not so soone found, as it was by them looked for, had
litle or no care of any other thing but to pamper their
bellies: or of that many which had litle understanding,
lesse discretion, and more tongue then was needfull or
requisite.

Some also were of a nice bringing up, only in cities
or townes, or such as never (as I may say) had seene

the world before. Because there were not to be found any English cities, nor such faire houses, nor at their owne wish any of their old accustomed dainty food, nor any soft beds of downe or feathers, the countrey was to them miserable, and their reports thereof according.

Because my purpose was but in briefe to open the cause of the variety of such speeches, the particularities of them, and of many envious, malicious, and slanderous reports and devices els, by our owne countreymen besides, as trifles that are not worthy of wise men to be thought upon, I meane not to trouble you withall, but will passe to the commodities, the substance of that which I have to make relation of unto you. . . . .

The conclusion.

Ow I have (as I hope) made relation not of so few and small things, but that the Countrey (of men that are indifferent and well disposed) may bee sufficiently liked: If there were no more knowen then I have mentioned, which doubtlesse and in great reason is nothing to that which remaineth to be discovered, neither the soyle, nor commodities. As we have reason so to gather by the difference we found in our travailes, for although al which I have before spoken of, have bene discovered and experimented not farre from the Sea coast, where was our abode and most of our travailing: yet sometimes as we made our journeys further into the maine and Countrey; we found the soile to be fatter, the trees greater and to grow thinner, the ground more firme and deeper mould, more and larger champions, finer grasse, and as good as ever we saw any in England; in some places rockie and farre more high and hilly ground, more plentie of their fruites, more abundance of beastes, the more inhabited with people, and of greater pollicie and larger dominions, with greater townes and houses. . . . .

A REPORT OF VIRGINIA

Seeing therefore the aire there is so temperate and holsome, the soyle so fertile, and yeelding such commodities, as I have before mentioned, the voyage also thither to and fro being sufficiently experimented to be perfourmed twise a yeere with ease, and at any season thereof: And the dealing of Sir Walter Ralegh so liberall in large giving and granting lande there, as is already knowen, with many helpes and furtherances else: (The least that he hath granted hath bene five hundreth acres to a man onely for the adventure of his person) I hope there remaines no cause whereby the action should be misliked.

If that those which shall thither travaile to inhabite and plant bee but reasonably provided for the first yeere, as those are which were transported the last, and being there, doe use but that diligence and care, that is requisit, and as they may with ease: There is no doubt, but for the time following, they may have victuals that are excellent good and plentie ynough, some more English sorts of cattel also hereafter, as some have bene before, and are there yet remayning, may, and shall be (God willing) thither transported. So likewise, our kinde of fruites, rootes, and hearbes, may be there planted and sowed, as some have bene already, and prove well: And in short time also they may raise so much of those sorts of commodities which I have spoken of, as shall both enrich themselves, as also others that shall deale with them. ....

JOHN WHITE'S

with the

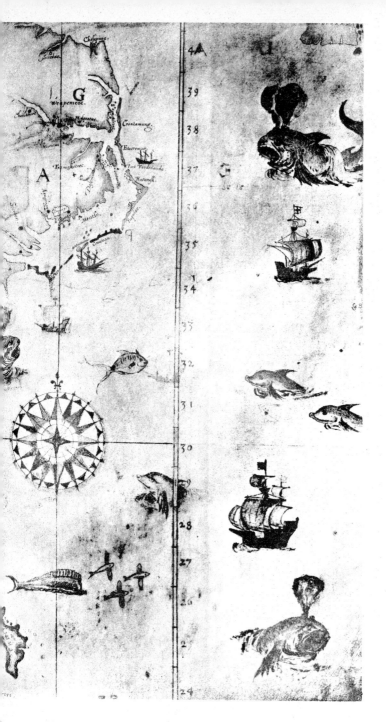

EAST COAST

aleigh

VIRGINIA 1584-1607

John White's Report

THE FOURTH VOYAGE TO VIRGINIA

Notes to John White's Report

Ralegh was determined to persist in his efforts to plant a colony in Virginia. A new expedition was organised and on May 8th, 1587 a new contingent of one hundred and fifty colonists was sent across the Atlantic. They were under the orders of one John White who was to be the Governor, with twelve assistants, of "the city of Raleigh in Virginia." There were difficulties with the Indians almost at once and the settlers feared that their supplies were inadequate, so they prevailed upon their Governor to return to England for additional stores. This White did and he never saw any of the colonists alive again. Here is John White's story.

The fourth voyage made to Virginia with three ships, in the yere 1587. Wherein was transported the second Colonie.

IN the yeere of our Lord 1587. Sir Walter Ralegh intending to persevere in the planting of his Countrey of Virginia, prepared a newe Colonie of one hundred and fiftie men to be sent thither, under the charge of John White, whom hee appointed Governour, and also appointed unto him twelve Assistants, unto whom hee gave a Charter, and incorporated them by the name of Governour and Assistants of the Citie of Ralegh in Virginia.

WE went the old course by the west Indies, and Simon Ferdinando our continuall Pilot mistaking Virginia for Cape Fear, we sayled not much to have beene cast away, upon the conceit of our all-knowing Ferdinando, had it not beene prevented by the vigilancy of Captaine Stafford. We came to Hatorask the 22. of July, and with fortie of our best men, intending at Roanoack to find the 50 men left by Sir Richard Grenvill. But we found nothing but the bones of a man, and where

the Plantation had beene, the houses unhurt, but overgrowne with weeds, and the Fort defaced, which much
perplexed us.

By the History it seemes Simon Ferdinando did what
he could to bring this voyage to confusion; but yet
they all arrived at Hatorask. They repayred the old
houses at Roanock, and Master George How, one of the
Councell, stragling abroad, was slaine by the Salvages.
Not long after Master Stafford with 20. men went to
Croatan with Manteo, whose friends dwelled there: of
whom we thought to have some newes of our 50 men.
They at first made shew to fight, but when they heard
Manteo, they threw away their Armes, and were friends,
and desired there might be a token given to be knowne
by, least we might hurt them by misprision, as the yeare
before one had bin by Master Layne, that was ever their
friend, and there present yet lame.

The next day we had conference with them concerning
the people of Secotan, Aquascogoc, and Pomeiok, willing
them of Croatan to see if they would accept friendship,
and renew our old acquaintance: which they willingly
imbraced, and promised to bring their King and Governours to Roanoak, to confirme it. We also understood
that Master Howe was slaine by the men of Wingina,
of Dassamonpeack: and by them of Roanoack, that the
fiftie men left by Sir Richard Grenvill, were suddainly
set upon by three hundred of Secotan, Aquascogoc, and
Dassamonpeack. First they intruded themselves among
11 of them by friendship, one they slew, the rest retyring
to their houses, they set them on fire, that our men with
what came next to hand were forced to make their passage
among them; where one of them was shot in the mouth,
and presently dyed, and a Salvage slaine by him. On
both sides more were hurt; but our men retyring to the
water side, got their boat, & ere they had rowed a quarter
of a myle towards Hatorask, they tooke up foure of their
fellowes, gathering Crabs and Oysters: at last they landed
on a little Ile by Hatorask, where they remained a while,

A NOBLEWOMAN OF POMEIOCK

A CHIEF OF ROANOKE

but after departed they knew not whether. So taking our leaves of the Croatans, we came to our Fleet at Hatorask.

The Governour having long expected the King and Governours of Pomeiok, Secotan, Aquascogoc, and Dassamonpeack, and the 7. dayes expired, and no newes of them, being also informed by those of Croatan, that they of Dassamonpeack slew Master How, and were at the driving our men from Roanoack he thought no longer to deferre the revenge. Wherefore about midnight, with Captaine Stafford, and twentie-foure men, whereof Manteo was one, for our guide, (that behaved himselfe towards us as a most faithfull English man) he set forward.

The next day by breake of day we landed, and got beyond their houses, where seeing them sit by the fire we assaulted them. The miserable soules amazed fled into the Reeds, where one was shot through, and we thought to have beene fully revenged, but we were deceived, for they were our friends come from Croatan to gather their corne, because they understood our enemies were fled after the death of Master How, and left all behinde them for the birds. But they had like to have payd too deare for it, had we not chanced upon a Weroances wife, with a childe at her backe, and a Salvage that knew Captaine Stafford, that ran to him calling him by his name. Being thus disappointed of our purpose, we gathered the fruit we found ripe, left the rest unspoyled, and tooke Menatonon his wife with her childe, and the rest with us to Roanoak. Though this mistake grieved Manteo, yet he imputed it to their own folly, because they had not kept promise to come to the governor at the day appointed. The 13. of August our Salvage Manteo was Christened, and called Lord of Dassamonpeack, in reward of his faithfulnesse. And the 18th, Ellinor the Governours daughter, and wife to Ananias Dare, was delivered of a daughter in Roanoak; which being the first Christian there borne, was called Virginia.

THE FOURTH VOYAGE TO VIRGINIA

Our ships being ready to depart, such a storme arose, as the Admirall was forced to cut her Cables: and it was six dayes ere she could recover the shore, that made us doubt she had beene lost, because the most of her best men were on shore. At this time Controversies did grow betwixt our Governour and the Assistants, about choosing one of them 12. to goe as Factor for them all to England; for all refused save one, whom all men thought most insufficient: the Conclusion was by a generall consent, they would have the Governour goe himselfe, for that they thought none would so truly procure there supplyes as he. Which though he did what he could to excuse it, yet their importunitie would not cease till he undertooke it, and had it under all their hands how unwilling he was, but that necessity and reason did doubly constraine him. At their setting sayle for England, waighing Anchor, twelve of the men in the flyboat were throwne from the Capstern, by the breaking of a barre, and most of them so hurt, that some never recovered it. The second time they had the like fortune, being but 15. they cut the Cable and kept company with their Admirall to Flowres and Corvos; the Admirall stayed there looking for purchase: but the flyboats men grew so weake they were driven to Smerwick in the West of Ireland. The Governour went for England; and Simon Ferdinando with much adoe at last arrived at Portsmouth. 1587.

The Names of those were landed in this Plantation were,

John White, Governour.	John Samson.
Roger Bayley.	Thomas Smith.
Ananias Dare.	Dionis Harvie.
Simon Ferdinando.	Roger Prat.
Christopher Couper.	George How.
Thomas Stevens.	Antony Cage.

With divers others to the number of about 115.

CHIEF LADIES OF SECOTAN

HOW THE CHIEF LADIES

DRESS AND CARRY THEIR CHILDREN

To the Worshipful and my very friend Master Richard Hakluyt, much happinesse in the Lord.

Ir, as well for the satisfying of your earnest request, as the performance of my promise made unto you at my last being with you in England, I have sent you (although in a homely stile, especially for the contentation of a delicate eare) the true discourse of my last voyage into the West Indies, and partes of America called Virginia, taken in hand about the end of Februarie, in the yeare of our redemption 1590. And what events happened unto us in this our journey, you shall plainely perceive by the sequele of my discourse. There were at the time aforesaid three ships absolutely determined to goe for the West Indies, at the speciall charges of M. John Wattes of London Marchant. But when they were fully furnished, and in readinesse to make their departure, a generall stay was commanded of all ships thorowout England. Which so soone as I heard, I presently (as I thought it most requisite) acquainted Sir Walter Ralegh therewith, desiring him that as I had sundry times afore bene chargeable and troublesome unto him, for the supplies and reliefes of the planters in Virginia : so likewise, that by his endevour it would please him at that instant to procure license for those three ships to proceede on with their determined voyage, that thereby the people in Virginia (if it were God's pleasure) might speedily be comforted and relieved without further charges unto him. Whereupon he by his good meanes obtained license of the Queenes Majestie, and order to be taken, that the owner of the 3 ships should be bound unto Sir Walter Ralegh or his assignes, in 3000 pounds, that those 3 ships in consideration of their release-

ment should take in, & transport a convenient number of passengers, with their furnitures and necessaries to be landed in Virginia. Neverthelesse that order was not observed, neither was the bond taken according to the intention aforesaid. But rather in contempt of the aforesaid order, I was by the owner and Commanders of the ships denied to have any passengers, or any thing els transported in any of the said ships, saving only my selfe & my chest; no not so much as a boy to attend upon me, although I made great sute, & earnest intreatie aswell to the chiefe Commanders, as to the owner of the said ships. Which crosse and unkind dealing, although it very much discontented me, notwithstanding the scarsity of time was such, that I could have no opportunity to go unto Sir Walter Ralegh with complaint : for the ships being then all in readinesse to goe to the Sea, would have bene departed before I could have made my returne. Thus both Governors, Masters, and sailers, regarding very smally the good of their countreymen in Virginia ; determined nothing lesse then to touch at those places, but wholly disposed themselves to seeke after purchase & spoiles, spending so much time therein, that sommer was spent before we arrived at Virginia. And when we were come thither, the season was so unfit, & weather so foule, that we were constrained of force to forsake that coast, having not seene any of our planters, with losse of one of our ship-boates, and 7 of our chiefest men : and also with losse of 3 of our ankers and cables, and most of our caskes with fresh water left on shore, not possible to be had aboord. Which evils & unfortunate events (as wel to their owne losse as to the hinderance of the planters in Virginia) had not chanced, if the order set downe by Sir Walter Ralegh had bene observed, or if my dayly & continuall petitions for the performance of the same might have taken any place. Thus may you plainely perceive the successe of my fift & last voiage to Virginia, which was no lesse unfortunately ended then frowardly begun, and as lucklesse to many, as sinister to my selfe. But I would to God it had bene as prosperous to all, as noysome to the planters ; & as joyfull to me, as discomfortable to them. Yet seeing it is not my first crossed voyage, I remaine contented. And wanting my wishes, I leave off from prosecuting that whereunto I would to God my wealth were answerable to my will. Thus committing the reliefe of my discomfortable company the planters in Virginia, to the merciful help of the Almighty, whom I most humbly beseech to helpe & comfort them, according to his most holy will & their good desire, I take my leave : from my house at Newtowne in Kylmore the 4 of February, 1593.

Your most welwishing friend,

JOHN WHITE.

The fift Voyage to Virginia ; undertaken by Mr. John White. 1589.

THe 20. of March three ships went from Plimouth, and passed betwixt Barbary and Mogadoro to Dominico in the West Indies. After we had done some exployts in those parts, the third of August wee fell with the low sandy Iles westward of Wokokon. But by reason of ill weather it was the 11. ere we could Anchor there ; and on the 12. we came to Croatan, where is a great breach in 35 degrees and a halfe, in the Northeast poynt of the Ile. The 15. we came to Hatorask in 36. degrees & a terse, at 4. fadom, 3 leagues from shore : where we might perceive a smoake at the place where I left the Colony, 1587. The next morning Captaine Cooke, Captaine Spicer, & their companies, with two boats left our ships, and discharged some Ordnance to give them notice of our comming, but when we came there, we found no man, nor signe of any that had beene there lately : and so returned to our Boats. · The next morning we prepared againe for Roanoack. Captaine Spicer had then sent his Boat ashore for water, so it was ten of the Clocke ere we put from the ships, which rode two myles from the shore. The Admirals boat, being a myle before the other, as she passed the bar, a sea broke into the boat and filled her halfe full of water : but by Gods good will, and the carefull stearage of Captaine Cook, though our provisions were much wet we safe escaped, the wind blew hard at Northeast, which caused so great a current and a breach upon the barre ; Captaine Spicer passed halfe over, but by the indiscreet steering of Ralph Skinner, their boat was overset, the men that could catch hold hung about her, the next sea cast her on ground, where some let goe their hold to wade to shore, but the sea beat them downe. The boat thus tossed up and downe Captaine Spicer and Skinner hung there till they were drowned ; but 4. that could swim a little, kept themselves in deeper water, were saved by the meanes of Captaine

THE FIFTH VOYAGE TO VIRGINIA

Cook, that presently upon the oversetting of their boat, shipped himselfe to save what he could. Thus of eleven, seven of the chiefest were drowned. This so discomfited all the Saylers, we had much to do to get them any more to seeke further for the Planters, but by their Captaines forwardnes at last they fitted themselves againe for Hatorask in 2 boats, with 19 persons. It was late ere we arrived, but seeing a fire through the woods, we sounded a Trumpet, but no answer could we heare. The next morning we went to it, but could see nothing but the grasse, and some rotten trees burning. We went up and downe the Ile, and at last found three faire Romane Letters carved. C.R.O. which presently we knew to signifie the place where I should find them, according to a secret note betweene them & me: which was to write the name of the place they would be in, upon some tree, dore, or post: and if they had beene in any distresse, to signifie it by making a crosse over it. For at my departure they intended to goe fiftie myles into the mayne. But we found no signe of distresse; then we went to a place where they were left in sundry houses, but we found them all taken downe, and the place strongly inclosed with a high Palizado, very Fortlike; and in one of the chiefe Posts carved in fayre capitall Letters CROATAN, without any signe of distresse, and many barres of Iron, two pigs of Lead, foure Fowlers, Iron shot, and such like heavie things throwne here and there, overgrowne with grasse and weeds. We went by the shore to seeke for their boats but could find none, nor any of the Ordnance I left them. At last some of the Sailers found divers Chists had beene hidden and digged up againe, and much of the goods spoyled, and scattered up and downe, which when I saw, I knew three of them to be my owne; but bookes, pictures, and all things els were spoyled. Though it much grieved me, yet it did much comfort me that I did know they were at Croatan; so we returned to our Ships, but had like to have bin cast away by a great storme that continued all that night.

69

The next morning we weighed Anchor for Croatan: having the Anchor a-pike, the Cable broke, by the meanes whereof we lost another: letting fall the third, the ship yet went so fast a drift, we fayled not much there to have split. But God bringing us into deeper water; considering we had but one Anchor, and our provision neare spent, we resolved to goe forthwith to S. Johns Ile, Hispaniola, or Trinidado, to refresh our selves and seeke for purchase that Winter, and the next Spring come againe to seeke our Country-men. But our Vice Admirall would not, but went directly for England, and we our course for Trinidado. But within two dayes after, the wind changing, we were constrained for the Westerne Iles to refresh our selves, where we met with many of the Queenes ships our owne consort, and divers others, the 23. of September 1590. And thus we left seeking our Colony, that was never any of them found, nor seene to this day 1622. And this was the conclusion of this Plantation, after so much time, labour, and charge consumed. Whereby we see;

Not all at once, nor all alike, nor ever hath it beene,
That God doth offer and confer his blessings upon men.

Written by Master John White.

A briefe Relation of the Description of Elizabeths
Ile, and some others towards the North part of
Virginia ; and what els they discovered in the
yeare 1602. by Captaine Bartholomew Gosnoll,
and Captaine Bartholomew Gilbert ; and divers
other Gentlemen their Associates.

ALL hopes of Virginia thus abandoned, it
lay dead and obscured from 1590. till
this yeare 1602. that Captaine Gosnoll,
with 32. and himselfe in a small Barke,
set sayle from Dartmouth upon the 26.
of March. Though the wind favoured
us not at the first, but force us as far
Southward as the Asores, which was not much out of
our way ; we ran directly west from thence, whereby
we made our journey shorter then heretofore by 500.
leagues : the weaknesse of our ship, the badnes of our
saylers, and our ignorance of the coast, caused us carry
but a low sayle, that made our passage longer then we
expected.

On fryday the 11. of May we made land, it was somewhat low, where appeared certaine hummocks or hills in
it : the shore white sand, but very rockie, yet overgrowne
with fayre trees. Comming to an Anchor, 8 Indians in
a Baske shallop, with mast and sayle came boldly aboord
us. It seemed by their signes & such things as they had,
some Biskiners had fished there : being about the latitude
of 43. But the harbour being naught, & doubting the
weather, we went not ashore, but waighed, and stood to
the Southward into the Sea. The next morning we
found our selves imbayed with a mightie headland : within
a league of the shore we anchored, and Captaine Gosnoll,
my selfe, & three others went to it in our boat, being a
white sand & a bold coast. Though the weather was hot,
we marched to the highest hils we could see, where we
perceived this headland part of the mayn, neare invironed

with Ilands. As we were returning to our ship, a good proper, lusty young man came to us, with whom we had but small conference, and so we left him. Here in 5. or 6. houres we tooke more Cod then we knew what to doe with, which made us perswade our selves, there might be found a good fishing in March, Aprill, and May.

At length we came among these fayre Iles, some a league, 2. 3. 5. or 6. from the Mayne, by one of them we anchored. We found it foure myles in compasse, without house or inhabitant. In it is a lake neare a myle in circuit; the rest overgrowne with trees, which so well as the bushes, were so overgrowne with Vines, we could scarce passe them. And by the blossomes we might perceive there would be plenty of Strawberries, Respises, Gousberries, and divers other fruits: besides, Deere and other Beasts we saw, and Cranes, Hernes, with divers other sorts of fowle; which made us call it Martha's Vineyard.

The rest of the Iles are replenished with such like; very rocky, and much tinctured stone like Minerall. Though we met many Indians, yet we could not see their habitations: they gave us fish, Tobacco, and such things as they had. But the next Isle we arrived at was but two leagues from the Maine, & 16. myle about, invironed so with creekes and coves, it seemed like many Isles linked together by small passages like bridges. In it is many places of plaine grasse, and such other fruits, and berries as before were mentioned. In mid-May we did sow Wheat, Barley, Oates, & Pease, which in 14. dayes sprung up 9. inches. The soyle is fat and lusty: the crust thereof gray, a foot or lesse in depth. It is full of high timbred Okes, their leaves thrise so broad as ours: Cedar straight and tall, Beech, Holly, Walnut, Hazell, Cherry trees like ours, but the stalke beareth the blossom or fruit thereof like a cluster of Grapes, forty or fiftie in a bunch. There is a tree of Orange colour, whose barke in the filing is as smooth as Velvet. There is a lake of fresh water three myles in compasse, in the midst an Isle containing an acre or thereabout, overgrowne with wood: here are many Tortoises, and abundance of all sorts of foules, whose young ones we tooke and eate at our pleasure. Grounds nuts as big as egges, as good as Potatoes, and 40. on a string, not two ynches under ground. All sorts of shell-fish, as Schalops, Mussels, Cockles, Crabs, Lobsters, Welks, Oysters, exceeding good and very great; but not to cloy you with particulars, what God and nature hath bestowed on those places, I refer you to the Authors owne writing at large. We called this Isle Elizabeths Isle, from whence we went right over to the mayne, where we stood a while as ravished at the beautie and dilicacy of the sweetnesse, besides divers cleare lakes, whereof we saw no end, & meadows very large and full of greene grasse, &c.

Here we espyed 7. Salvages, at first they expressed some feare, but by our courteous usage of them, they followed us to the necke of Land, which we thought had beene severed from the Mayne, but we found it otherwise. Here we imagined was a river, but because the day was farre spent, we left to discover it till better leasure. But of good Harbours, there is no doubt, considering the Land is all rocky and broken lands. The next day we determined to fortifie our selves in the Isle in the lake. Three weekes we spent in building us there a house. But the second day after our comming from the Mayne, 11. Canows with neare 50. Salvages came towards us. Being unwilling they should see our building, we went to, & exchanged with them Knives, Hatchets, Beades, Bels, and such trifles, for some Bevers, Lyzards, Martins, Foxes, wilde Catte skinnes, and such like. We saw them have much red Copper, whereof they make chaines, collars, and drinking cups, which they so little esteemed they would give us for small toyes, & signified unto us they had it out of the earth in the Mayne: three dayes they stayed with us, but every night retyred two or three myle from us: after with many signes of love and friendship they departed, seaven of them staying behind, that did helpe us to dig and carry Saxafras, and doe any thing they could, being of a comely proportion and the best condition of any Salvages we had yet incountred. They have no Beards but counterfeits, as they did thinke ours also was: for which they would have changed with some of our men that had great beards. Some of the baser sort would steale; but the better sort, we found very civill and just. We saw but three of their women, and they were but of meane stature, attyred in skins like the men, but fat and well favoured. The wholesomenesse and temperature of this climate, doth not onely argue the people to be answerable to this Description, but also of a perfect constitution of body, active, strong, healthfull, and very witty, as the sundry toyes by them so cunningly wrought may well testifie. For our selves, we found our selves rather increase in health and strength then otherwise; for all our toyle, bad dyet and lodging; yet not one of us was touched with any sicknesse. Twelve intended here a while to have stayed, but upon better consideration, how meanely we were provided, we left this Island (with as many true sorrowfull eyes as were before desirous to see it) the 18. of June, and arrived at Exmouth, the 23 of July.

But yet mans minde doth such it selfe explay,
As Gods great Will doth frame it every way.
And, Such thoughts men have, on earth that doe but live,
As men may crave, but God doth onely give.

Written by John Brierton one of the Voyage.

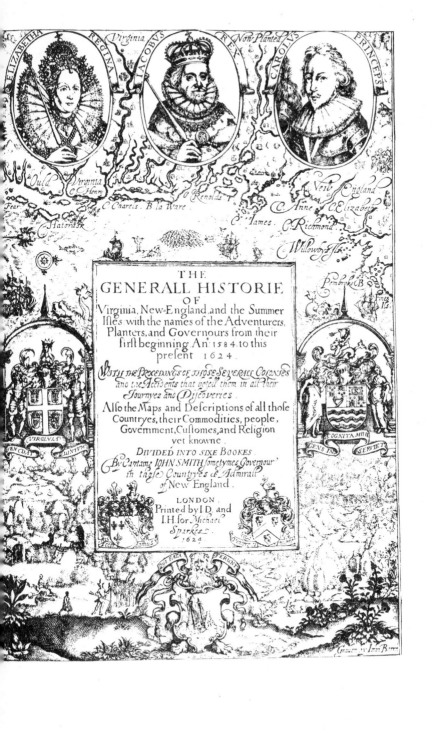

ELIZABETHA REGINA   Virginia   IACOBVS REX   Now Planted   CAROLVS PRINCEPS

Ould Virginia   C. Henry
Fear   C. Chares. B. la Ware   O Renolds
Hatorask   C. James.   C. Richmond
New England
C. Anne   C. Elizabeth
Willowby Hz.

Pembrook B.
Fines Is.

THE
GENERALL HISTORIE
OF
Virginia, New-England, and the Summer
Isles with the names of the Adventurers,
Planters, and Governours from their
first beginning An° 1584. to this
present 1624.

WITH THE PROCEEDINGS OF THOSE SEVERALL COLONIES
and the Accidents that befell them in all their
Journyes and Discoveries.

Also the Maps and Descriptions of all those
Countryes, their Commodities, people,
Government, Customes, and Religion
yet knowne.

DIVIDED INTO SIXE BOOKES.

By Captaine IOHN SMITH sometymes Governour
in those Countryes & Admirall
of New England.

LONDON.
Printed by I.D. and
I.H. for Michael
Sparkes.
1624.

VIRGVLA   GENS INCOGNITA MIHI SERVIET

James Town 1607

Jamestown was capital of Virginia for 92 years, i.e. from 1607 to 1699 when the capital was moved to Williamsburg which was named after King William.

In 1799, the capital was again moved, this time to Richmond.

JAMES TOWN

1607

ARELY have three small ships carried such a burden of destiny as did the "Susan Constant", the "Godspeed", and the "Discovery" when in 1607 they finally set out upon their momentous voyage across the Atlantic. Many times before, ships and men had been sent across those wide waters to the far land of Virginia—but this was different. The ships of Captains Newport, Ratliffe and Gosnoll were carrying not another forlorn hope, as perhaps many of those who sailed in them feared in their secret hearts, but the men and women who were to bring birth to a new nation.

Jamestown Island was the chosen place of landing. Here, thirteen years before the arrival of the Pilgrims at Plymouth, English people made their first permanent settlement in the New World. The venture was no haphazard one. Careful arrangement had been made for the government of the new colony before the ships set sail. A Board of seven Councillors was to be set up—Wingfield, a veteran of the wars in the Low Countries, Captains Gosnoll, Newport, and Ratliffe; Martin, who has served under Drake; John Smith, and George Kendall, a relative of Sir Edwin Sandys, prominent in the Virginia Company.

Others prominent in the new colony were George Percy, handsome son of the Earl of Northumberland and the chronicler of the early days of the pioneers, Gabriel Archer, an early explorer of New England, and the Rev. Robert Hunt whose piety and devotion was an inspiration to all.

From the very moment they landed these gallant few were exposed to almost incredible hardships. New supplies of men and food were sent out by the Company until the population reached about five hundred. Then came the starving time. The winter of 1609-10 Percy, then President of the Council wrote: '. . . We were glad to make shifts with vermin, as dogs, cats, rats, and mice . . . to search the woods and feed upon serpents and snakes and to dig the earth for wild and unknown roots . . . Nothing was spared to maintain life . . .' In May 1610 there were only sixty survivors welcoming the relief ship of Sir Thomas Gates, himself a survivor of shipwreck in Bermuda. Gates found life in Jamestown at a very low ebb. The town itself seemed 'rather as the ruins of some ancient fortification, than any people living might now inhabit it . . . The Indian as fast killing without as the famine and pestilence within'. Gates surveyed the scene and decided that the colony ought to be abandoned.

English North America, not for the first time, was at the cross road of destiny. The survivors embarked with Gates and set off down the James. While still in the river they got the stirring news that Lord Delaware, sent out by the Company as the colony's new Governor, was off point Comfort with 150 men and ample supplies. The ships stood in the river. Slowly they turned about and sailed up-stream ahead of Delaware's fleet. Jamestown got its people again. North America was to be an English speaking nation.

Notes to Captain John Smith

If Raleigh was the spiritual father of Virginia, John Smith was its material founder. Born in the little Lincolnshire village of Willoughby in 1580 he pursued an adventurous career, being successively a soldier in the low Countries, a free-lance in Hungary—where he killed the hordes of pagans who supply the three severed heads on his coat of arms—and then a captive and slave of the Turks. When the three ships of the 'Jamestown' colonists entered Hampton Roads and opened their sealed orders from the Company, they found that Smith had been nominated a member of the colony's Board of Governors. He was at that moment chained up below decks. On the voyage he had become intolerable to the others as a fault finder and trouble maker. Smith was released but told he could not sit on the Council.

Conditions in the young colony were such as he thrived on. In the first six months the original one hundred and four settlers had been reduced to thirty-eight. They died of "swellings, fluxes, burning fevers and by wars; some departed suddenly, but for the most part they died of mere famine." "Their bodies trailed out of their cabins like dogs to be buried." Within the year Smith was the accepted leader of the colony. He supplied the extra drive and initiative the others seemed to lack, but which they needed so badly in order to survive the rigors of cold, pestilence, warfare and starvation.

Before he had been in the colony much more than two years he was injured in a gunpowder accident and came back to England. The Company never employed him again and he never went back to Virginia. Smith, though supremely capable, was a difficult man. Here are excerpts from his book "The Generall Historie of Virginia, New England and The Summer Isles".

The Proceedings

And Accidents of The English Colony in Virginia, Extracted from the Authors following, by William Simons, Doctour of Divinitie.

T might well be thought, a Countrie so faire (as Virginia is) and a people so tractable, would long ere this have beene quietly possessed, to the satisfaction of the adventurers, & the eternizing of the memory of those that effected it. But because all the world doe see a defailement; this following Treatise shall give satisfaction to all indifferent Readers, how the businesse hath bin carried : where no doubt they will easily understand and answer to their question, how it came to passe there was no better speed and successe in those proceedings.

Captaine Bartholomew Gosnoll, one of the first movers of this plantation, having many yeares solicited many of his friends, but found small assistants; at last prevailed with some Gentlemen, as Captaine John Smith, Mr. Edward-maria Wingfield, Mr. Robert Hunt, and divers others, who depended a yeare upon his projects, but nothing could be effected, till by their great charge and industrie, it came to be apprehended by certaine of the Nobilitie, Gentry, and Marchants, so that his Majestie by his letters patents, gave commission for establishing Councels, to direct here; and to governe, and to execute there. To effect this, was spent another yeare, and by that, three ships were provided, one of 100 Tuns, another of 40. and a Pinnace of 20. The transportation of the company was committed to Captaine Christopher Newport, a Marriner well practised for the Westerne parts of America. But their orders for government were put in a box, not to be opened, nor the governours knowne untill they arrived in Virginia.

On the 19 of December, 1606. we set sayle from Blackwall, but by unprosperous winds, were kept six weekes in the sight of England; all which time, Mr. Hunt our Preacher, was so weake and sicke, that few expected his recovery. Yet although he were but twentie myles from his habitation (the time we were in the Downes) and notwithstanding the stormy weather, nor the scandalous imputations (of some few, little better then Atheists, of the greatest ranke amongst us) suggested against him, all this could never force from him so much as a seeming desire to leave the busines, but preferred the service of God, in so good a voyage, before any affection to contest with his godlesse foes, whose disasterous designes (could they have prevailed) had even then overthrowne the businesse, so many discontents did then arise, had he not with the water of patience, and his godly exhortations (but chiefly by his true devoted examples) quenched those flames of envie, and dissention.

We watered at the Canaries, we traded with the Salvages at Dominica; three weekes we spent in refreshing our selves amongst these west-India Isles; in Gwardalupa we found a bath so hot, as in it we boyled Porck as well as over the fire. And at a little Isle called Monica, we tooke from the bushes with our hands, neare two hogsheads full of Birds in three or foure houres. In Mevis,

Mona, and the Virgin Isles, we spent some time, where, with a lothsome beast like a Crocodil, called a Gwayn, Tortoises, Pellicans, Parrots, and fishes, we daily feasted. Gone from thence in search of Virginia, the company was not a little discomforted, seeing the Marriners had 3 dayes passed their reckoning and found no land, so that Captaine Ratliffe (Captaine of the Pinnace) rather desired to beare up the helme to returne for England, then make further search. But God the guider of all good actions, forcing them by an extreame storme to hull all night, did drive them by his providence to their desired Port, beyond all their expectations, for never any of them had seene that coast. The first land they made they called Cape Henry; where thirtie of them recreating themselves on shore, were assaulted by five Salvages, who hurt two of the English very dangerously. That night was the box opened, and the orders read, in which Bartholomew Gosnoll, John Smith, Edward Wingfield, Christopher Newport, John Ratliffe, John Martin, and George Kendall, were named to be the Councell, and to choose a President amongst them for a yeare, who with the Councell should governe. Matters of moment were to be examined by a Jury, but determined by the major part of the Councell, in which the President had two voyces. Untill the 13 of May they sought a place to plant in, then the Councell was sworne, Mr. Wingfield was chosen President, and an Oration made, why Captaine Smith was not admitted of the Councell as the rest.

Now falleth every man to worke, the Councell contrive the Fort, the rest cut downe trees to make place to pitch their Tents; some provide clapbord to relade the ships, some make gardens, some nets, &c. The Salvages often visited us kindly. The Presidents overweening jealousie would admit no exercise at armes, or fortification, but the boughs of trees cast together in the forme of a halfe moone by the extraordinary paines and diligence of Captaine Kendall, Newport, Smith, and twentie others, were sent to discover the head of the river: by divers small habitations they passed, in six dayes they arrived at a Towne called Powhatan, consisting of some twelve houses, pleasantly seated on a hill; before it three fertile Isles, about it many of their cornefields, the place is very pleasant, and strong by nature, of this place the Prince is called Powhatan, and his people Powhatans, to this place the river is navigable: but higher within a myle, by reason of the Rockes and Isles, there is not passage for a small Boat, this they call the Falles, the people in all parts kindly intreated them, till being returned within twentie myles of James towne, they gave just cause of jealousie, but had God not blessed the discoverers otherwise then those at the Fort, there had then beene an end of that plantation; for at the Fort, where they arrived the next day, they found 17 men hurt, and a boy slaine by the Salvages, and had it not chanced a crosse barre shot from the Ships strooke down a bough from a tree amongst them, that caused them to retire, our men had all beene slaine, being securely all at worke, and their armes in dry fats.

Hereupon the President was contented the Fort should be pallisadoed, the Ordnance mounted, his men armed and exercised, for many were the assaults, and ambuscadoes of the Salvages, & our men by their disorderly stragling were often hurt, when the Salvages by the nimblenesse of their heeles well escaped. What toyle we had, with so small a power to guard our workemen adayes, watch all night, resist our enemies, and effect our businesse, to relade the ships, cut downe trees, and prepare the ground to plant our Corne, &c, I referre to the Readers consideration. Six weekes being spent in this manner, Captaine Newport (who was hired onely for our transportation) was to returne with the ships. Now Captaine Smith, who all this time from their departure from the Canaries was restrained as a prisoner upon the scandalous suggestions of some of the chiefe (envying his repute) who fained he intended to usurpe the government, murther the Councell, and make himselfe King, that his confederats were dispersed in all the three ships, and that divers of his confederats that revealed it, would affirme it, for this he was committed as a prisoner: thirteene weekes he remained thus suspected, and by that time the ships should returne they pretended out of their commisserations, to referre him to the Councell in England to receive a check, rather then by particulating his designes make him so odious to the world, as to touch his life, or utterly overthrow his reputation. But he so much scorned their charitie, and publikely defied the uttermost of their crueltie, he wisely prevented their policies, though he could not suppresse their envies, yet so well he demeaned himselfe in this businesse, as all the company did see his innocency, and his adversaries malice, and those suborned to accuse him, accused his accusers of subornation; many untruthes were alledged against him; but being so apparently disproved, begat a generall hatred in the hearts of the company against such unjust Commanders, that the President was adjudged to give him 200l. so that all he had was seized upon, in part of satisfaction, which Smith presently returned to the Store for the generall use of the Colony. Many were the mischiefes that daily sprung from their ignorant (yet ambitious) spirits; but the good Doctrine and exhortation of our Preacher Mr. Hunt reconciled them, and caused Captaine Smith to be admitted of the Councell; the next day all received the Communion, the day following the Salvages voluntarily desired peace, and Captaine Newport returned for England with newes; leaving in Virginia 100. the 15 of June 1607. . . . .

Eing thus left to our fortunes, it fortuned that within ten dayes scarce ten amongst us could either goe, or well stand, such extreame weaknes and sicknes oppressed us. And thereat none need marvaile, if they consider the cause and reason, which was this; whilest the ships stayed, our allowance was somewhat bettered, by a daily proportion

of Bisket, which the sailers would pilfer to sell, give, or exchange with us, for money, Saxefras, furres, or love. But when they departed, there remained neither taverne, beere house, nor place of reliefe, but the common Kettell. Had we beene as free from all sinnes as gluttony, and drunkennesse, we might have beene canonized for Saints; But our President would never have beene admitted, for ingrossing to his private, Oatmeale, Sacke, Oyle, Aquavitæ, **Beefe, Egges, or what not, but the Kettell; that indeed he allowed equally to be distributed, and that was halfe a pint of wheat, and as much barley boyled with water for a man a day, and this having fryed some 26. weekes in the ships hold, contained as many wormes as graines; so that we might truely call it rather so much bran then corne, our drinke was water, our lodgings Castles in the ayre: with this lodging and dyet, our extreame toile in bearing and planting Pallisadoes, so strained and bruised us, and our continuall labour in the extremitie of the heat had so weakned us, as were cause sufficient to have made us as miserable in our native Countrey, or any other place in the world. From May, to September, those that escaped, lived upon Sturgeon, and Sea-crabs, fiftie in this time we buried, the rest seeing the Presidents projects to escape these miseries in our Pinnace by flight (who all this time had neither felt want nor sicknes) so moved our dead spirits, as we deposed him; and established Ratcliffe in his place, (Gosnoll being dead) Kendall deposed, Smith newly recovered, Martin and Ratcliffe was by his care preserved and relieved, and the most of the souldiers recovered, with the skilfull diligence of Mr. Thomas Wotton our Chirurgian generall. But now was all our provision spent, the Sturgeon gone, all helps abandoned, each houre expecting the fury of the Salvages; when God the patron of all good indevours, in that desperate extremitie so changed the hearts of the Salvages, that they brought such plenty of their fruits, and provision, as no man wanted. . . . .**

THE SORCERER

The new President and Martin, being little beloved, of weake judgement in dangers, and lesse industrie in peace, committed the managing of all things abroad to Captaine Smith: who by his owne example, good words, and faire promises, set some to mow, others to binde thatch, some to build houses, others to thatch them, himselfe alwayes bearing the greatest taske for his owne share, so that in short time, he provided most of them lodgings, neglecting any for himselfe. This done, seeing the Salvages superfluitie beginne to decrease (with some of his workemen) shipped himselfe in the Shallop to search the Country for trade. The want of the language, knowledge to mannage his boat without sailes, the want of a sufficient power, (knowing the multitude of the Salvages) apparell for his men, and other necessaries, were infinite impediments, yet no discouragement...................

And now the winter approaching, the rivers became so covered with swans, geese, duckes, and cranes, that we daily feasted with good bread, Virginia pease, pumpions, and putchamins, fish, fowle, and diverse sorts of wild beasts as far as we could eate them: so that none of our Tuftaffaty humorists desired to goe for England. But our Comædies never endured long without a Tragedie; some idle exceptions being muttered against Captaine Smith, for not discovering the head of Chickahamania river, and taxed by the Councell, to be too slow in so worthy an attempt. The next voyage hee proceeded so farre that with much labour by cutting of trees in sunder he made his passage, but when his Barge could passe no farther, he left her in a broad bay out of danger of shot, commanding none should goe a shore till his returne: himselfe with two English and two Salvages went up higher in a Canowe, but hee was not long absent, but his men went a shore, whose want of government, gave both occasion and opportunity to the Salvages to surprise one George Cassen, whom they slew, and much failed

not to have cut of the boat and all the rest.   Smith little
dreaming of that accident, being got to the marshes at
the rivers head, twentie myles in the desert, had his * two
men slaine (as is supposed) sleeping by the Canowe, whilst
himselfe by fowling sought them victuall, who finding he
was beset with 200. Salvages, two of them hee slew, still
defending himselfe with the ayd of a Salvage his guid,
whom he bound to his arme with his garters, and used
him as a buckler, yet he was shot in his thigh a little, and
had many arrowes that stucke in his cloathes but no great
hurt, till at last they tooke him prisoner.   When this
newes came to James towne, much was their sorrow for
his losse, fewe expecting what ensued.   Sixe or seven
weekes those Barbarians kept him prisoner, many strange
triumphes and conjurations they made of him, yet hee so
demeaned himselfe amongst them, as he not onely diverted
them from surprising the Fort, but procured his owne
libertie, and got himselfe and his company such estimation
amongst them, that those Salvages admired him more then
their owne Quiyouckosucks. . . . .

At last they brought him to Meronocomo, where was
Powhatan their Emperor.   Here more then two hundred
of those grim Courtiers stood wondering at him, as he
had beene a monster ; till Powhatan and his trayne had
put themselves in their greatest braveries.   Before a fire
upon a seat like a bedsted, he sat covered with a great
robe, made of Rarowcun skinnes, and all the tayles hanging by.   On either hand did sit a young wench of 16 or
18 yeares, and along on each side the house, two rowes of
men, and behind them as many women, with all their
heads and shoulders painted red ; many of their heads
bedecked with the white downe of Birds ; but every one
with something : and a great chayne of white beads about

Maſſaw-(*Maſſawomeck*) Lomecks

GINIA

1608

Signification of theſe marks,
To the croſſes hath bin diſcouered,
what beyond is by relation.
Kings houſes 2
Ordinary houſes 2

307

308

309

The Saſques-ahanougs
are a Gyant like peo-ple &
Vakange thus a-prell &

S A S Q V E
S A H A
O V G H

A R O V

Attaock

Tesinigh

Quadroque

Saſquiſahanough

N

Blands
C:

Downes dale

Capny

L BAY

Powels Iſt

Bernes point

Oxinies

Forest

Paynt Pcynce

Takonod Hu

Gunters Harbour

Peregrins mount

T O C K
W O G H S A

and halfe

Leames

Chickahokin

Maſscek

T I X E S

H V K E S

Atquanachuk

310

Diſcrib'd by Captayn John Smith
by William Hole

Page 43
Smith

their necks. At his entrance before the King, all the people gave a great shout. The Queene of Appamatuck was appointed to bring him water to wash his hands, and another brought him a bunch of feathers, in stead of a Towell to dry them: having feasted him after their best barbarous manner they could, a long consultation was held, but the conclusion was, two great stones were brought before Powhatan: then as many as could layd hands on him, dragged him to them, and thereon laid his head, and being ready with their clubs, to beate out his braines, Pocahontas the Kings dearest daughter, when no intreaty could prevaile, got his head in her armes, and laid her owne upon his to save him from death: whereat the Emperour was contented he should live to make him hatchets, and her bells, beads, and copper; for they thought him aswell of all occupations as themselves. For the King himselfe will make his owne robes, shooes, bowes, arrowes, pots; plant, hunt, or doe any thing so well as the rest.

The Pocahontas Story

In the Edward VI Grammar School at Louth, Lincolnshire (John Smith's old school) there is a mural depicting the celebrated episode in which the beautiful Pocahontas begs for the life of Smith from her father, Powhatan, who is about to order his execution.

Smith was captured by the Indians in December 1607. He did not tell anyone at Jamestown or elsewhere of the dramatic circumstances of his salvation until 1624, seventeen years later, when he wrote his "General History". In his early work "A True Relation of Virginia" he says nothing of it. Pocahontas was aged thirteen at the time of the alleged rescue and was well known in Jamestown. In 1614 she married John Rolfe, one of the Jamestown pioneers.

As Rebekah Rolfe she went to England with her husband in 1616 and "wore a hat and ruff and wielded a fan like a civilized fine lady." While she was in England John Smith presented himself to her as an old Jamestown acquaintance. Only with difficulty did she remember him. Pocahontas was in England for only one year before she died. "At her return towards Virginia," writes Purchas, "she came to Gravesend, to her end and grave, having given great demonstrations of her Christian sincerity, as the first fruits of Virginian conversion." She is buried in the Churchyard of St. George's, Gravesend. She left one son. Among others President Wilson's second wife traced her descent from him.

MATOAKA ALS REBECCA FILIA POTENTISS · PRINC · POWHATANI IMP · VIRGINIÆ · ✤ ·

Ætatis suæ 21. A̅.
1616.

Matoaks als Rebecka daughter to the mighty Prince
Powhatan Emperour of Attanoughskomouck als virginia
converted and baptized in the Christian faith, and
wife to the wor:ll Mr Joh: Rolff.

"The blessed Pocahontas, as the historian calls her. And great king's
daughter of Virginia." Ben Johnson: Staple of News, 1625.

The Copy of a Letter sent to the Treasurer and Councell of Virginia from Captaine Smith, then President in Virginia.

Right Honorable, &c.

I Received your Letter, wherein you write, that our minds are so set upon faction, and idle conceits in dividing the Country without your consents, and that we feed You but with ifs & ands, hopes, & some few proofes; as if we would keepe the mystery of the businesse to our selves: and that we must expresly follow your instructions sent by Captain Newport: the charge of whose voyage amounts to neare two thousand pounds, the which if we cannot defray by the Ships returne, we are like to remain as banished men. To these particulars I humbly intreat your Pardons if I offend you with my rude Answer.

For our factions, unlesse you would have me run away and leave the Country, I cannot prevent them: because I do make many stay that would els fly any whether. For the idle Letter sent to my Lord of Salisbury, by the President and his confederats, for dividing the Country &c. What it was I know not, for you saw no hand of mine to it; nor ever dream't I of any such matter. That we feed you with hopes, &c. Though I be no scholer, I am past a schoole-boy; and I desire but to know, what either you, and these here doe know, but that I have learned to tell you by the continuall hazard of my life. I have not concealed from you any thing I know; but I feare some cause you to beleeve much more then is true.

Expresly to follow your directions by Captaine Newport, though they be performed, I was directly against it; but according to our Commission, I was content to be over-ruled by the major part of the Councell, I feare to the hazard of us all; which now is generally confessed when it is too late. Onely Captaine Winne and Captaine Waldo I have sworne of the Councell, and Crowned Powhatan according to your instructions.

For the charge of this Voyage of two or three thousand pounds, we have not received the value of an hundred pounds. And for the quartred Boat to be borne by the Souldiers over the Falles, Newport had 120 of the best men he could chuse. If he had burnt her to ashes, one might have carried her in a bag, but as she is, five hundred cannot, to a navigable place above the Falles. And for him at that time to find in the South Sea, a Mine of gold; or any of them sent by Sir Walter Raleigh: at our Con-sultation I told them was as likely as the rest. But during this great discovery of thirtie myles, (which might as well have beene done by one man, and much more, for the value of a pound of Copper at a seasonable tyme) they had the Pinnace and all the Boats with them, but one that remained with me to serve the Fort. In their absence I followed the new begun workes of Pitch and Tarre, Glasse, Sope-ashes, and Clapboord, whereof some small quantities we have sent you. But if you rightly consider, what an infinite toyle it is in Russia and Swethland, where the woods are proper for naught els, and though there be the helpe both of man and beast in those ancient Common-wealths, which many an hundred yeares have used it, yet thousands of those poore people can scarce get necessaries to live, but from hand to mouth. And though your Factors there can buy as much in a week as will fraught you a ship, or as much as you please; you must not expect from us any such matter, which are but a many of ignorant miserable soules, that are scarce able to get wherewith to live, and defend our selves against the inconstant Salvages: finding but here and there a tree fit for the purpose, and want all things els the Russians have. For the Coronation of Powhatan, by whose advice you sent him such presents, I know not; but this give me leave to tell you, I feare they will be the confusion of us all ere we heare from you againe. At your Ships arrivall, the Salvages harvest was newly gathered, and we going to buy it, our owne not being halfe sufficient for so great a number. As for the two ships loading of Corne Newport promised to provide us from Powhatan, he brought us but foureteene Bushels; and from the Monacans nothing, but the most of the men sicke and neare famished. From your Ship we had not provision in victuals worth twenty pound, and we are more then two hundred to live upon this: the one halfe sicke, the other little better. For the Saylers (I confesse) they daily make good cheare, but our dyet is a little meale and water, and not sufficient of that. Though there be fish in the Sea, foules in the ayre, and Beasts in the woods, their bounds are so large, they so wilde, and we so weake and ignorant, we cannot much trouble them. Captaine Newport we much suspect to be the Authour of those inventions. Now that you should know, I have made you as great a discovery as he, for lesse charge then he spendeth you every meale; I have sent you this Mappe of the Bay and Rivers, with an annexed Relation of the Countries and Nations that inhabit them, as you may see at large. Also two barrels of stones, and such as I take to be good Iron ore at the least; so devided, as by their notes you may see in what places I found them. The Souldiers say many of your officers maintaine their families out of that you send us: and that Newport hath an hundred pounds a yeare for carrying newes. For every master you have yet sent can find the way as well as he, so that an hundred pounds might be spared, which is more then we have all, that helpe to pay him wages. Cap. Ratliffe is now called Sicklemore, a poore counterfeited imposture. I have sent you him home, least the company should cut his throat. What he is, now every one can tell you: if he and Archer returne againe, they are sufficient to keepe us alwayes in factions. When you send againe I intreat you rather send but thirty Carpenters, husbandmen, gardiners, fisher men, blacksmiths, masons, and diggers up of trees, roots, well provided; then a thousand of such as we have: for except wee be able both to lodge them, and feed them, the most will consume with want of necessaries before they can be made good for any thing. Thus if you please to consider this account, and of the unnecessary wages to Captaine Newport, or his ships so long lingering and staying here (for notwithstanding his boasting to leave us victuals for 12 moneths, though we had 89 by this discovery lame and sicke, and but a pinte of Corne a day for a man, we were constrained to give him three hogs-heads of that to victuall him homeward) or yet to send into Germany or Poleland for glasse-men & the rest, till we be able to sustaine our selves, and relieve them when they come. It were better to give five hundred pound a tun for those grosse Commodities in Denmarke, then send for them hither, till more necessary things be provided. For in over-toyling our weake and unskilfull bodies, to satisfie this desire of present profit, we can scarce ever recover our selves from one Supply to another. And I humbly intreat you hereafter, let us know what we should receive, and not stand to the Saylers courtesie to leave us what they please, els you may charge us with what you will, but we not you with any thing. These are the causes that have kept us in Virginia, from laying such a foundation, that ere this might have given much better content and satis-faction; but as yet you must not looke for any profitable returnes: so I humbly rest.

The Seal of
"His Majesties Council of Virginia"

To make Plaine

the True Proceedings of the Historie for 1609. we
must follow the examinations of Doctor
Simons, and two learned Orations published by the Companie; with
the relation of the Right
Honourable the Lord
De la Ware.

What happened in the first government after the
alteration in the time of Captaine George
Piercie their Governour.

He day before Captaine Smith returned for
England with the ships, Captaine Davis
arrived in a small Pinace, with some
sixteene proper men more: To these were
added a company from James towne,
under the command of Captaine John
Sickelmore alias Ratliffe, to inhabit Point
Comfort. Captaine Martin and Captaine West, having
lost their boats and neere halfe their men among the
Salvages, were returned to James towne; for the
Salvages no sooner understood Smith was gone, but they
all revolted, and did spoile and murther all they

97

I

incountered. Now wee were all constrained to live onely on that Smith had onely for his owne Companie, for the rest had consumed their proportions, and now they had twentie Presidents with all their appurtenances: Master Piercie our new President, was so sicke hee could neither goe nor stand. But ere all was consumed, Captaine West and Captaine Sickelmore, each with a small ship and thirtie or fortie men well appointed, sought abroad to trade. Sickelmore upon the confidence of Powhatan, with about thirtie others as carelesse as himselfe, were all slaine, onely Jeffrey Shortridge escaped, and Pokahontas the Kings daughter saved a boy called Henry Spilman, that lived many yeeres after, by her meanes, amongst the Patawomekes. Powhatan still as he found meanes, cut off their Boats, denied them trade, so that Captaine West set saile for England. Now we all found the losse of Captaine Smith, yea his greatest maligners could now curse his losse: as for corne, provision and contribution from the Salvages, we had nothing but mortall wounds, with clubs and arrowes; as for our Hogs, Hens, Goats, Sheepe, Horse, or what lived, our commanders, officers & Salvages daily consumed them, some small proportions sometimes we tasted, till all was devoured; then swords, armes, pieces, or any thing, wee traded with the Salvages, whose cruell fingers were so oft imbrewed in our blouds, that what by their crueltie, our Governours indiscretion, and the losse of our ships, of five hundred within six moneths after Captaine Smiths departure, there remained not past sixtie men, women and children, most miserable and poore creatures; and those were preserved for the most part, by roots, herbes, acornes, walnuts, berries, now and then a little fish: they that had startch in these extremities, made no small use of it; yea, even the very skinnes of our horses. Nay, so great was our famine, that a Salvage we slew, and buried, the poorer sort tooke him up againe and eat him, and so did divers one another boyled and stewed with roots and herbs: And one amongst the rest did kill his wife, powdered her, and had eaten part of her before it was knowne, for which hee was executed, as hee well deserved; now whether shee was better roasted, boyled or carbonado'd, I know not, but of such a dish as powdered wife I never heard of. This was that time, which still to this day we called the starving time; it were too vile to say, and scarce to be beleeved, what we endured: but the occasion was our owne, for want of providence, industrie and government, and not the barrennesse and defect of the Countrie, as is generally supposed; for till then in three yeeres, for the numbers were landed us, we had never from England provision sufficient for six moneths, though it seemed by the bils of loading sufficient was sent us, such a glutton is the Sea, and such good fellowes the Mariners; we as little tasted of the great proportion sent us, as they of our want and miseries, yet notwithstanding they ever over-swayed and ruled the businesse, though we endured all that is said, and chiefly lived on what this good Countrie naturally afforded; yet had wee beene even in Paradice it selfe with these Governours, it would not have beene much better with us; yet there was amongst us, who had they had the government as Captaine Smith appointed, but that they could not maintaine it, would surely have kept us from those extremities of miseries. This in ten daies more, would have supplanted us all with death.

But God that would not this Countrie should be unplanted, sent Sir Thomas Gates, and Sir George Sommers with one hundred and fiftie people most happily preserved by the Bermudas to preserve us: strange it is to say how miraculously they were preserved in a leaking ship, as at large you may reade in the insuing Historie of those Ilands.

The government resigned to Sir Thomas Gates, 1610.

WHen these two Noble Knights did see our miseries, being but strangers in that Countrie, and could understand no more of the cause, but by conjecture of our clamours and complaints, of accusing and excusing one another: They embarked us with themselves, with the best meanes they could, and abandoning James towne, set saile for England, whereby you may see the event of the government of the former Commanders left to themselves; although they had lived there many yeeres as formerly hath beene spoken (who hindred now their proceedings, Captaine Smith being gone.)

At noone they fell to the Ile of Hogs, and the next morning to Mulbery point, at what time they descried the Long-boat of the Lord la Ware, for God would not have it so abandoned. For this honourable Lord, then Governour of the Countrie, met them with three ships exceedingly well furnished with all necessaries fitting, who againe returned them to the abandoned James towne. Out of the observations of William Simmons Doctor of Divinitie.

The government devolved to the Lord la Ware.

HIs Lordship arrived the ninth of June 1610. accompanied with Sir Ferdinando Waynman, Captaine Houlcroft, Captaine Lawson, and divers other Gentlemen of sort; the tenth he came up with his fleet, went on shore, heard a Sermon, read his Commission, and entred into consultation for the good of the Colonie, in which secret counsell we will a little leave them, that we may duly observe the revealed counsell of God. Hee that shall but turne up his eie, and behold the spangled canopie of heaven, or shall but cast downe his eie, and consider the embroydered carpet of the earth, and withall shall marke how the heavens heare the earth, and the earth the Corne and Oile, and they relieve the necessities of man, that man will acknowledge Gods infinite providence: But hee that shall further observe, how God inclineth all casuall events to worke the necessary helpe of his Saints, must needs adore the Lords infinite goodnesse; never had any people more just cause, to cast themselves at the very foot-stoole of God, and to reverence his mercie, than this distressed Colonie; for if God had not sent Sir Thomas

Gates from the Bermudas, within foure daies they had almost beene famished; if God had not directed the heart of that noble Knight to save the Fort from fiering at their shipping, for many were very importunate to have burnt it, they had beene destitute of a present harbour and succour; if they had abandoned the Fort any longer time, and had not so soone returned, questionlesse the Indians would have destroied the Fort, which had beene the meanes of our safeties amongst them and a terror. If they had set saile sooner, and had lanched into the vast Ocean, who would have promised they should have incountered the Fleet of the Lord la Ware, especially when they made for New found land, as they intended, a course contrarie to our Navie approaching. If the Lord la Ware had not brought with him a yeeres provision, what comfort would those poore soules have received, to have beene relanded to a second distruction? This was the arme of the Lord of Hosts, who would have his people passe the red Sea and Wildernesse, and then to possesse the land of Canaan.

Epilogue

Raleigh was the man who pointed the way. Despite his many changes of fortune, he never lost his interest in, or concern for, Virginia. In thirteen years, from 1589 to 1602, he made five vain attempts to locate and relieve the colony he had planted. In 1607, when a prisoner in the Tower of London, he begged Queen Anne, the wife of James I, to get permission for him to join the Jamestown venture, and the same year he sent out his nephew Ralph Gilbert, because he himself was not permitted to sail. However, he lived to hear of the delivery of Jamestown and is rightly honoured as the true founder of Virginia.

Next to him John Smith must be remembered; he led the young colony in its most difficult days and saw it win through. But what are leaders without the men of mettle, the women of character who follow behind them? What are dreams without the men who can make them reality? Jamestown had suffered disease, famine, and attack. A population of five hundred settlers had shrunk to one of sixty. Subjected to every kind of physical and mental torment a savage continent could offer, they stood the test.

The base of the Tower on the Jamestown Festival grounds bears the inscription:

1607

AT JAMESTOWN BEGAN

THE

EXPANSION OVERSEAS OF THE

ENGLISH SPEAKING PEOPLES;

THE

COMMONWEALTH OF VIRGINIA;

THE

UNITED STATES OF AMERICA;

THE

BRITISH COMMONWEALTH OF NATIONS,

1957

APPENDIX

RALEIGH CAPTURES A SPANISH GOVERNOR

NOTES TO RALEIGH   John Aubrey

I have now forgott whether Sir Walter Raleigh was not for the putting of Mary Queen of Scotts to death ; I thinke, yea : but besides that, at a consultation at Whitehall after Queen Elizabeth's death, how matters were to be ordered and what ought to be donne, Sir Walter Raleigh declared his opinion, 'twas the wisest way for them to keepe the Government in their owne hands and sett up a Commonwealth, and not to be subject to a needy, beggarly nation. It seems there were some of this caball who kept this not so secret but that it came to King James' eare, who, where the English Noblesse mett and received him, being told upon presentment to his Majesty their names, when Sir Walter Raleigh's name was told (Ralegh) said the King, O my soule, mon, I have heard rawly of thee.

It was a most stately sight, the glory of that Reception of his Majesty, where the Nobility and Gentry were in exceeding rich equippage, having enjoyed a long peace under the most excellent of Queens : and the Company was so exceeding numerous that their obedience carried a secret dread with it. King James did not inwardly like it, and, with an inward envy, sayd that he doubted not but that he should have been able on his owne strength (should the English have kept him out) to have dealt with them, and get his Right. Sayd Sir Walter Raleigh to him, Would to God that had been putt to the tryall : Why doe you wish that sayd the King. Because, sayd Sir Walter ; that then you would have known your friends from your foes. But that reason of Sir Walter was never forgotten nor forgiven.

Even such is tyme that takes in Trust
Our Youth, our Joyes, our all we have,
And payes us but with Earth and Dust ;
Who, in the darke and silent Grave,

When we have wandered all our wayes
Shutts up the Story of our Dayes.
But from this Earth, this Grave, this Dust,
My God shall rayse me up I trust.

These Lines Sir Walter Raleigh wrote in his Bible, the night before he was beheaded, and desired his Relations with these words, viz. *beg my dead body, which living is denyed you ; and bury it either in Sherbourne or Exeter Church.* He was somtimes a Poet, not often.

A Scaffold was erected in the old Palace yard, upon which after 14 yeares reprivement, his head was cutt off : at which time, such abundance of bloud issued from his veines, that shewed he had stock of nature enough left to have continued him many yeares in life, though now above three score yeares old, if it had not been taken away by the hand of Violence. And this was the end of the great Sir Walter Raleigh : great sometimes in the favour of Queen Elizabeth, and next to Sir Francis Drake, the great Scourge and hate of the Spaniard, who had many things to be commended in his life, but none more than his constancy at his death, which he tooke with so undaunted a resolution that one might perceive that he had a certain expectation of a better life after it, so far he was from holding those Atheisticall opinions, an Aspersion whereof some had cast upon him.

TOBACCO

Thomas Hariot

There is an herbe which is sowed apart by it selfe, and is called by the inhabitants Uppowoc: in the West Indies it hath divers names, according to the severall places and countreys where it groweth and is used: the Spanyards generally call it Tabacco. The leaves thereof being dried and brought into pouder, they use to take the fume or smoake thereof, by sucking it thorow pipes made of clay, into their stomacke and head; from whence it purgeth superfluous fleame and other grosse humours, and openeth all the pores and passages of the body: by which meanes the use thereof not onely preserveth the body from obstructions, but also (if any be, so that they have not bene of too long continuance) in short time breaketh them: whereby their bodies are notably preserved in health, and know not many grievous diseases, wherewithall we in England are often times afflicted.

This Uppowoc is of so precious estimation amongst them, that they thinke their gods are marvellously delighted therewith: whereupon sometime they make hallowed fires, and cast some of the pouder therin for a sacrifice: being in a storme upon the waters, to pacifie their gods, they cast some up into the aire and into the water: so a weare for fish being newly set up, they cast some therein and into the aire: also after an escape of danger, they cast some into the aire likewise: but all done with strange gestures, stamping, sometime dancing, clapping of hands, holding up of hands, and staring up into the heavens, uttering therewithall, and chattering strange words and noises.

We our selves, during the time we were there, used to sucke it after their maner, as also since our returne, and have found many rare and woonderfull experiments of the vertues thereof: of which the relation would require a volume by it selfe: the use of it by so many of late men and women of great calling, as els, and some learned Physicians also, is sufficient witnesse.

VIRGINIA 1584-1607

John Smith

To the most high and vertuous Princesse Queene Anne of Great Brittanie.

Most admired Queene,

THe love I beare my God, my King and Countrie, hath so oft emboldened mee in the worst of extreme dangers, that now honestie doth constraine mee presume thus farre beyond my selfe, to present your Majestie this short discourse : if ingratitude be a deadly poyson to all honest vertues, I must bee guiltie of that crime if I should omit any meanes to bee thankfull. So it is,

That some ten yeeres agoe being in Virginia, and taken prisoner by the power of Powhatan their chiefe King, I received from this great Salvage exceeding great courtesie, especially from his sonne Nantaquans, the most manliest, comeliest, boldest spirit, I ever saw in a Salvage, and his sister Pocahontas, the Kings most deare and wel-beloved daughter, being but a childe of twelve or thirteene yeeres of age, whose compassionate pitifull heart, of my desperate estate, gave me much cause to respect her : I being the first Christian this proud King and his grim attendants ever saw : and thus inthralled in their barbarous power, I cannot say I felt the least occasion of want that was in the power of those my mortall foes to prevent, notwithstanding al their threats. After some six weeks fatting amongst those Salvage Courtiers, at the minute of my execution, she hazarded the beating out of her owne braines to save mine, and not onely that, but so prevailed with her father, that I was safely conducted to James towne, where I found about eight and thirtie miserable poore and sicke creatures, to keepe possession of all those large territories of Virginia, such was the weaknesse of this poore Commonwealth, as had the Salvages not fed us, we directly had starved.

And this reliefe, most gracious Queene, was commonly brought us by this Lady Pocahontas, notwithstanding all these passages when inconstant Fortune turned our peace to warre, this tender Virgin would still not spare to dare to visit us, and by her our jarres have beene oft appeased, and our wants still supplyed; were it the policie of her father thus to imploy her, or the ordinance of God thus to make her his instrument, or her extraordinarie affection to our Nation, I know not: but of this I am sure; when her father with the utmost of his policie and power, sought to surprize mee, having but eighteene with mee, the darke night could not affright her from comming through the irkesome woods, and with watered eies gave me intelligence, with her best advice to escape his furie; which had hee knowne, hee had surely slaine her. James towne with her wild traine she as freely frequented, as her fathers habitation; and during the time of two or three yeeres, she next under God, was still the instrument to preserve this Colonie from death, famine and utter confusion, which if in those times had once beene dissolved, Virginia might have line as it was at our first arrivall to this day. Since then, this businesse having beene turned and varied by many accidents from that I left it at: it is most certaine, after a long and troublesome warre after my departure, betwixt her father and our Colonie, all which time shee was not heard of, about two yeeres after shee her selfe was taken prisoner, being so detained neere two yeeres longer, the Colonie by that meanes was relieved, peace concluded, and at last rejecting her barbarous condition, was maried to an English Gentleman, with whom at this present she is in England; the first Christian ever of that Nation, the first Virginian ever spake English, or had a childe in mariage by an Englishman, a matter surely, if my meaning bee truly considered and well understood, worthy a Princes understanding.

Round Robin from Walloon Emigrants

An interesting light on the origin of the State of New York and its connection with the Settlement in Virginia is thrown by this

Promise, in the form of a Round Robin, by certain Walloons and French to go and inhabit Virginia, a land under the obedience of the King of Great Britain. (July 1621) French. Twenty-nine signatures and twenty-seven marks in lieu of signatures.

A Round Robin is a petition or declaration in which the signatures are arranged in a circle so as to disguise the order in which the subscribers have signed *to avoid prosecution of the instigator*. The reason for its use on this occasion is not clear. The project appears to have failed owing to the failure of the English Government to provide shipping. The leader, Jesse de Forest (whose signature appears on the left hand side, just above the middle) was more successful with the Dutch West India Company, and founded New Amsterdam (now New York) in 1623. Presumably the Walloon and French settlers who accompanied him on that occasion included most of the signatories to this document.

Public Record Office,
London.

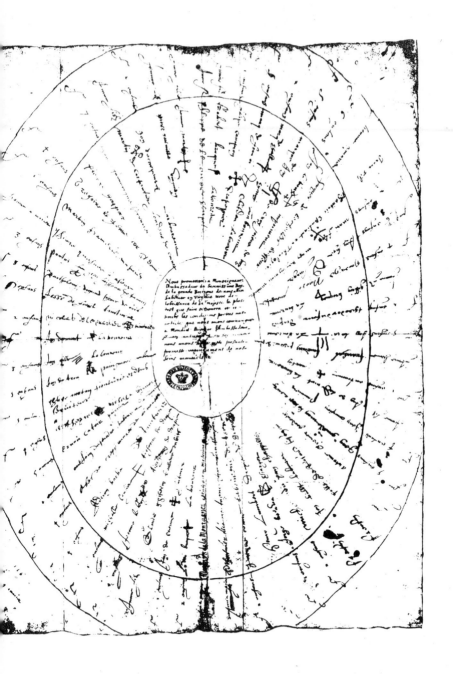

VOCABULARY

John Smith

Because many doe desire to know the manner of their Language, I have inserted these few words.

KA katorawinos yowo. What call you this.

Nemarough, a man.

Grenepo, a woman.

Marowanchesso, a boy.

Yehawkans, Houses.

Matchcores, Skins, or garments.

Mockasins, Shooes.

Tussan, Beds.

Pokatawer, Fire.

Attawp, A bow.

Attonce, Arrowes.

Monacookes, Swords.

Aumouhhowgh, A Target.

Pawcussacks, Gunnes.

Tomahacks, Axes.

Tockahacks, Pickaxes.

Pamesacks, Knives.

Accowprets, Sheares.

Pawpecones, Pipes.

Mattassin, Copper.

Ussawassin, Iron, Brass, Silver, or any white mettall.

Musses, Woods.

Attasskuss, Leaves, weeds, or grasse.

Chepsin, Land.

Maskapow, the worst of the enemies.

Mawchick chammay, The best of friends.

Casacunnakack, peya quagh acquintan uttasantasough, In how many daies will there come hither any more English Ships.

Okees, Gods.

Quiyoughcosoughs, Pettie Gods, and their affinities.

Righcomoughes, Deaths.

Kekughes, Lives.

Mowchick woyawgh tawgh noeragh kaqueremecher, I am very hungry? what shall I eate?

VOCABULARY

Shacquohocan, A stone.
Wepenter, A cookold.
Suckahanna, Water.
Noughmass, Fish.
Copotone, Sturgeon.
Weghshaughes, Flesh.
Sawwehone, Bloud.
Netoppew, Friends.
Marrapough, Enemies.

Tawnor nehiegh Powhatan, Where dwels Powhatan.
Mache, nehiegh yourowgh, Orapaks, Now he dwels a great way hence at Orapaks.
Vittapitchewayne anpechitchs nehawper Werowacomoco, You lie, he staid ever at Werowacomoco.
Kator nehiegh mattagh neer uttapitchewayne, Truely he is there I doe not lie.
Spaughtynere keragh werowance mawmarinough kekaten wawgh peyaquaugh, Run you then to the King Mawmarynough and bid him come hither.

Their Numbers.
Necut, 1. Ningh, 2. Nuff, 3. Yowgh, 4. Paranske, 5. Comotinch, 6. Toppawoss, 7. Nusswash, 8, Kekatawgh, 9. Kaskeke, 10.
They count no more but by tennes as followeth.
Case, how many.
Ninghsapooeksku, 20.
Nussapooeksku, 30.
Yowghapooeksku, 40.
Parankestassapooeksku, 50.
Comatinchtassapooeksku, 60.
Nussswashtassapooeksku, 70.
Kekataughtassapooeksku, 90.

Necuttoughtysinough, 100.
Necuttweunquaough, 1000.

Rawcosowghs, Dayes.
Keskowghes, Sunnes.
Toppquough, Nights.
Nepawweshowghs, Moones.
Pawpaxsoughes, Yeares.
Pummahumps, Starres.
Osies, Heavens.

Utteke, e peya weyack wighwhip, Get you gone, & come againe quickly.
Kekaten Pokahontas patiaquagh niugh tanks manotyens neer mowchick rawrenock audowgh, Bid Pokahontas bring hither two little Baskets, and I will give her white Beads to make her a Chaine.

FAMOUS VIRGINIANS

George Washington

Thomas Jefferson

James Madison

James Munroe

Presidents of the United States